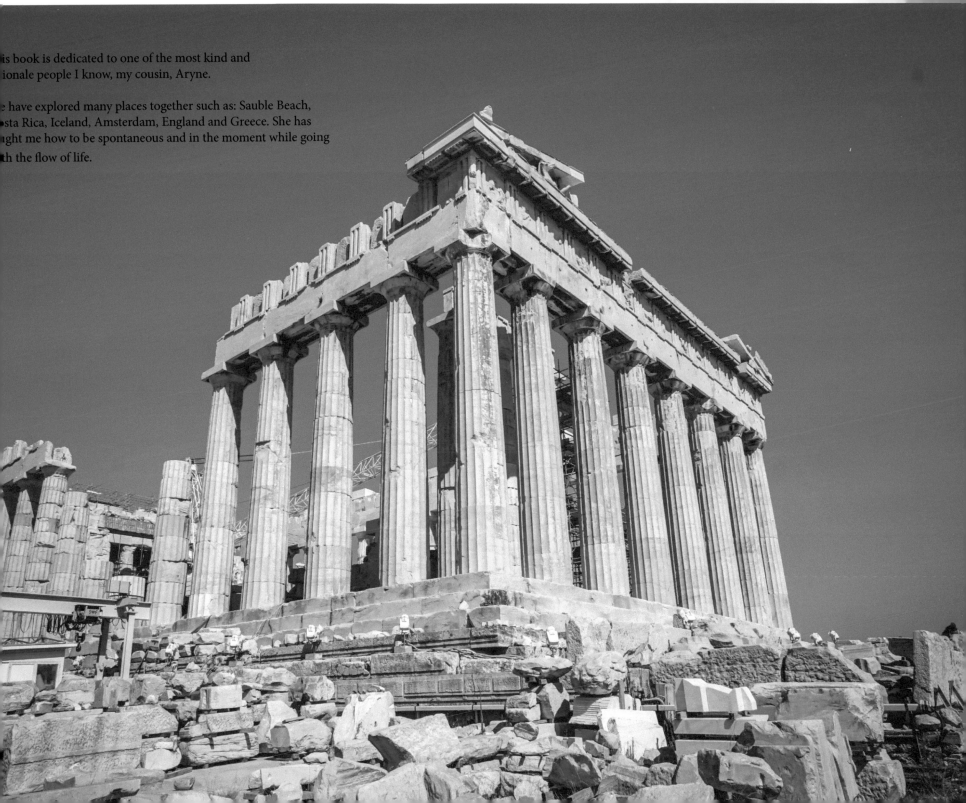

This book is dedicated to one of the most kind and
rationale people I know, my cousin, Aryne.

We have explored many places together such as: Sauble Beach,
Costa Rica, Iceland, Amsterdam, England and Greece. She has
taught me how to be spontaneous and in the moment while going
with the flow of life.

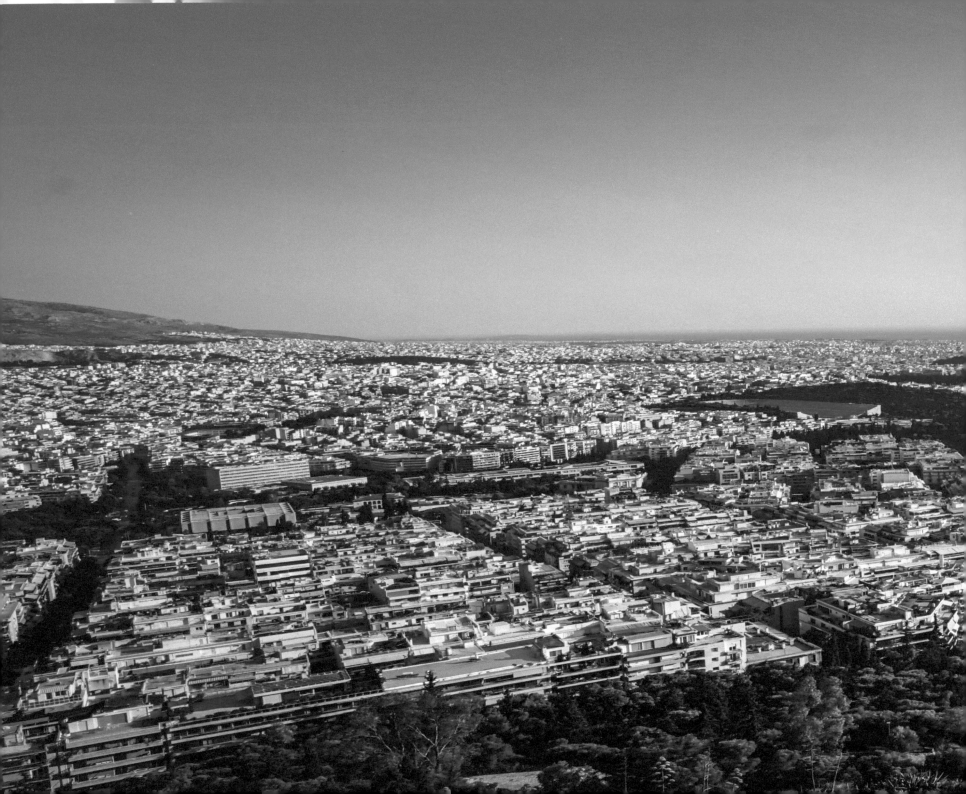

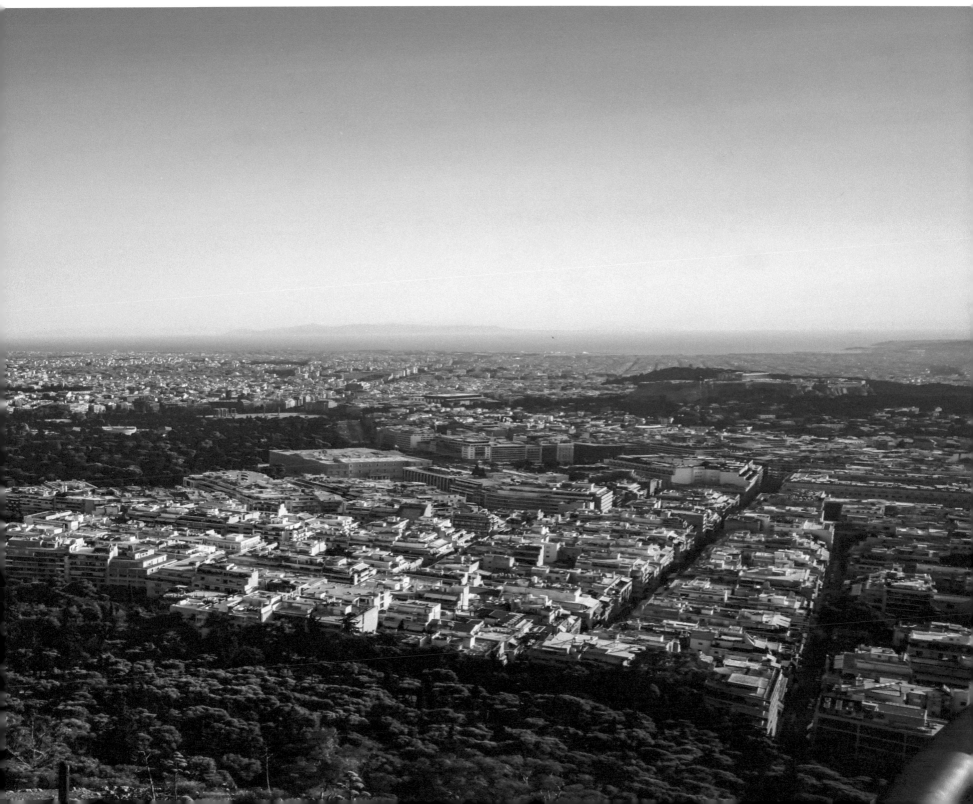

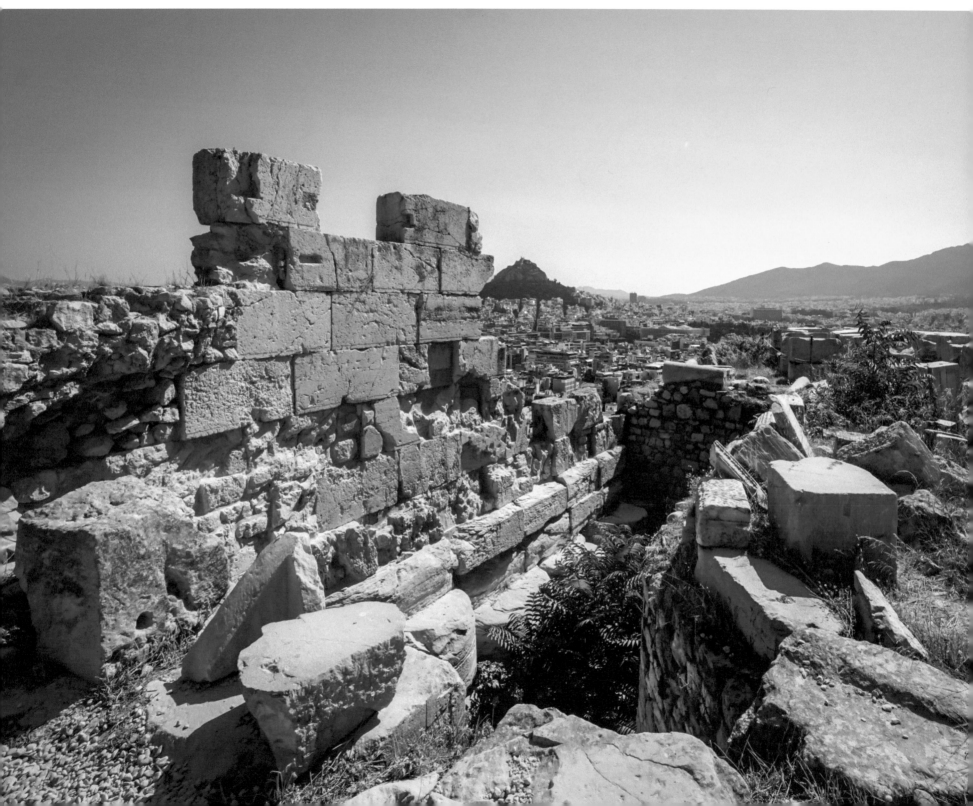

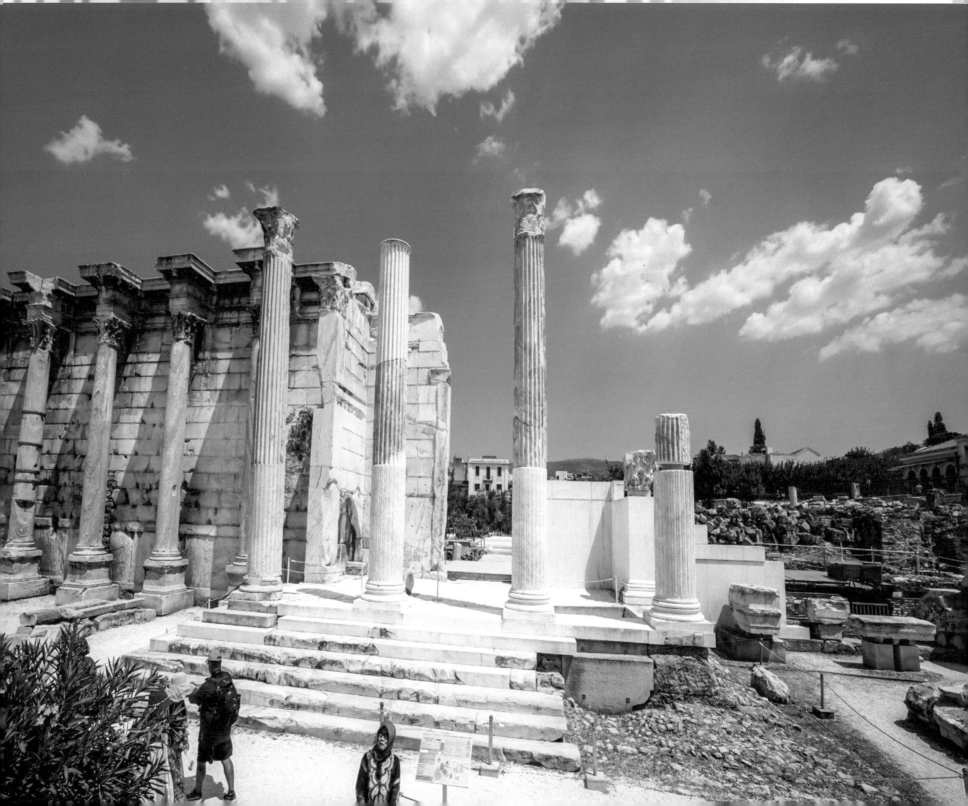

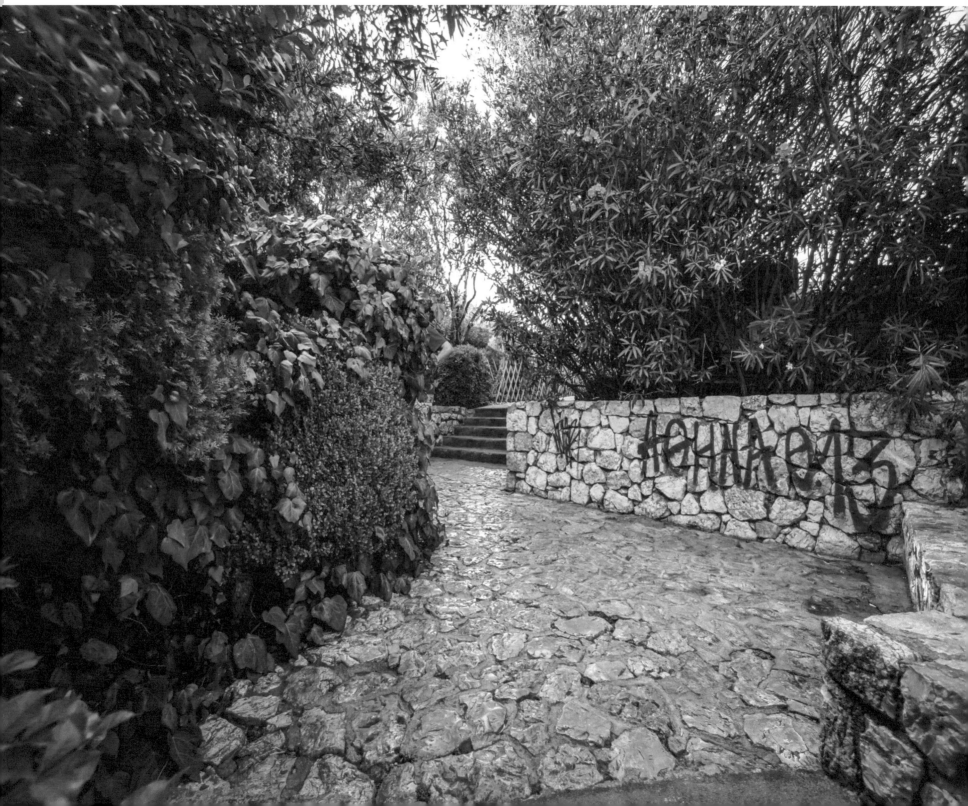

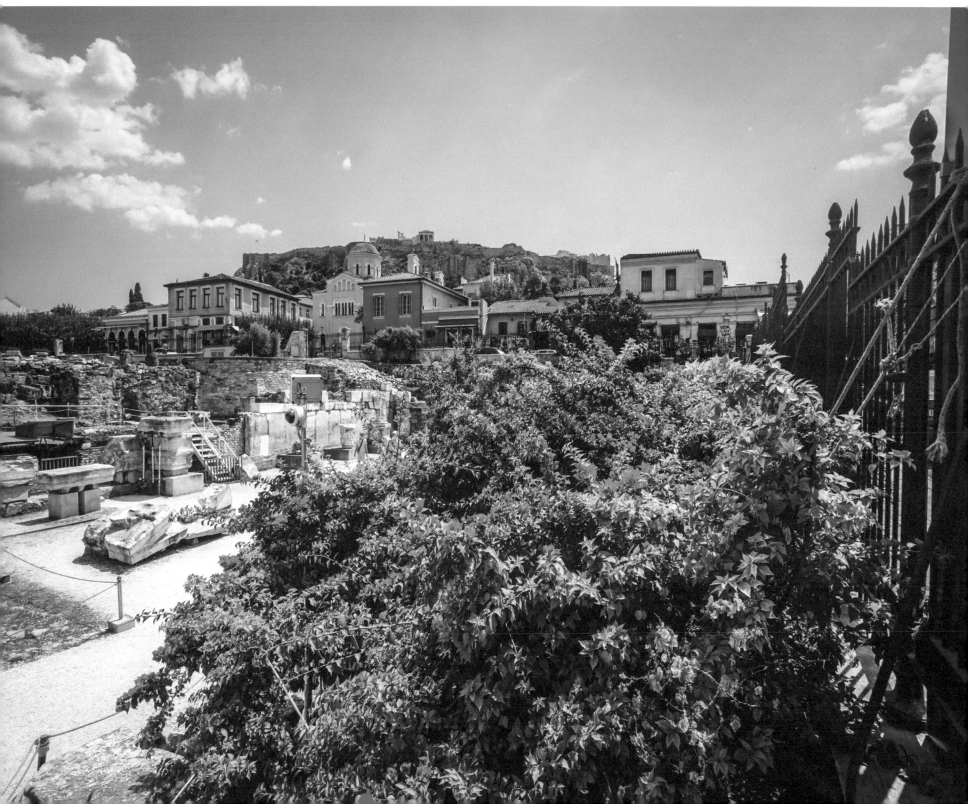

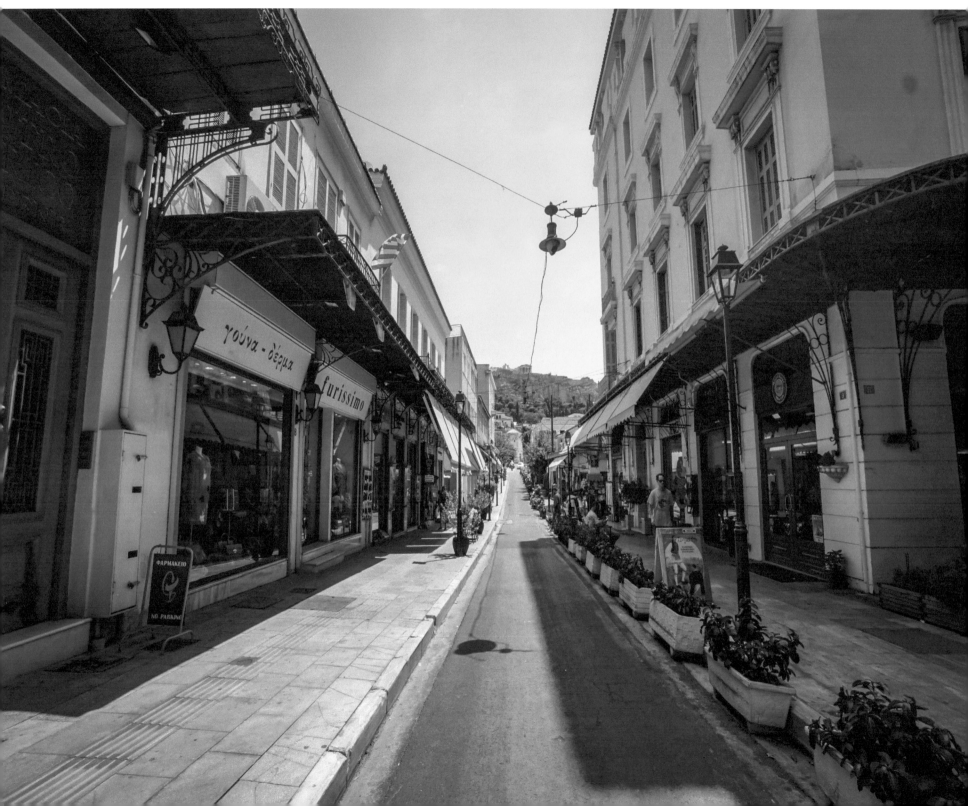

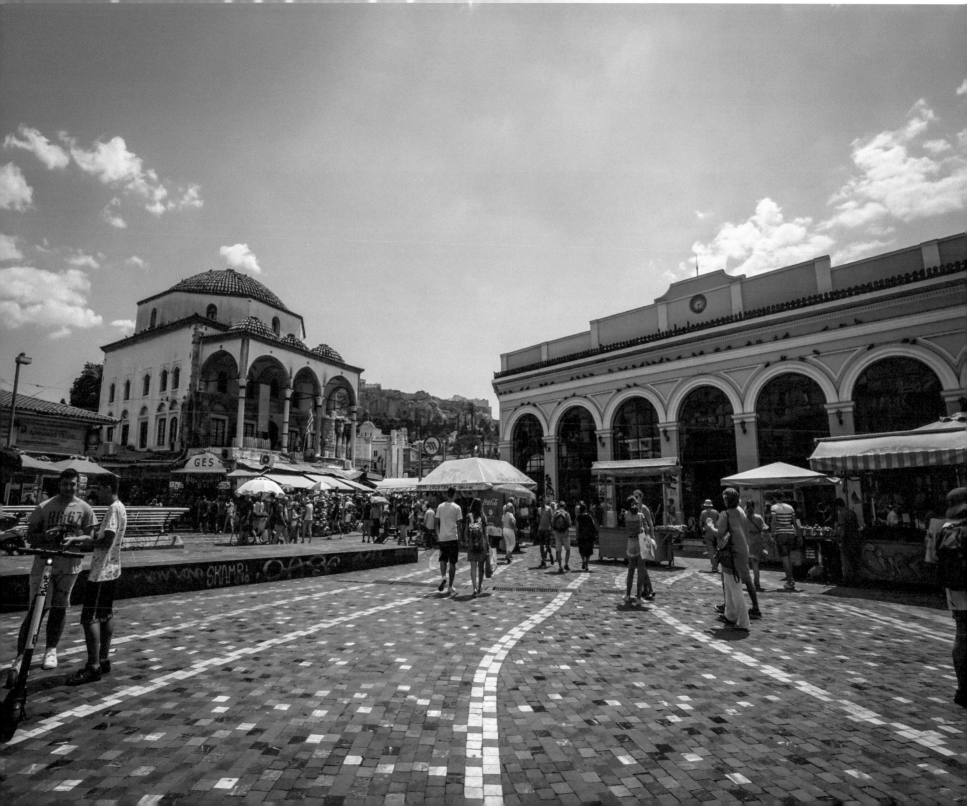

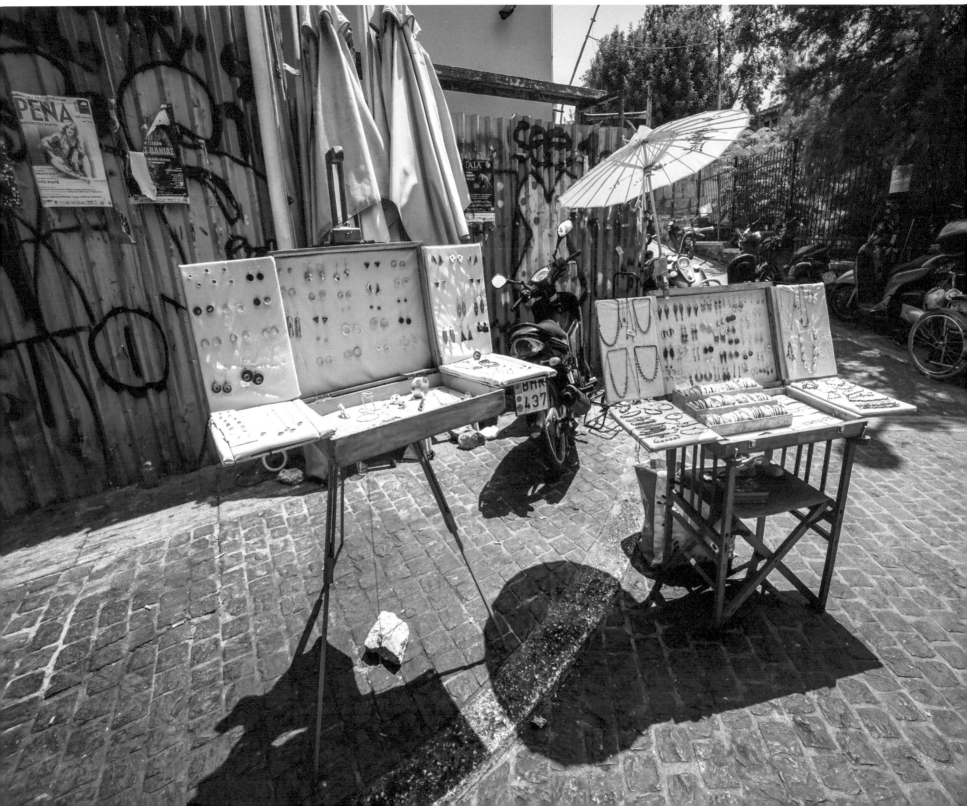

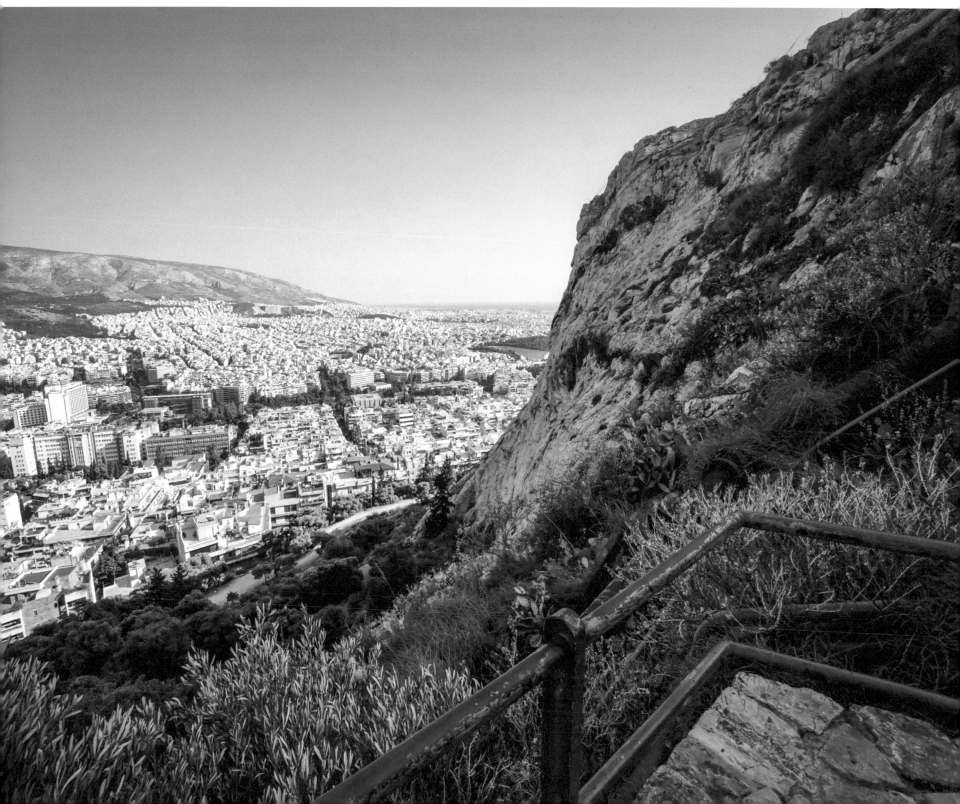

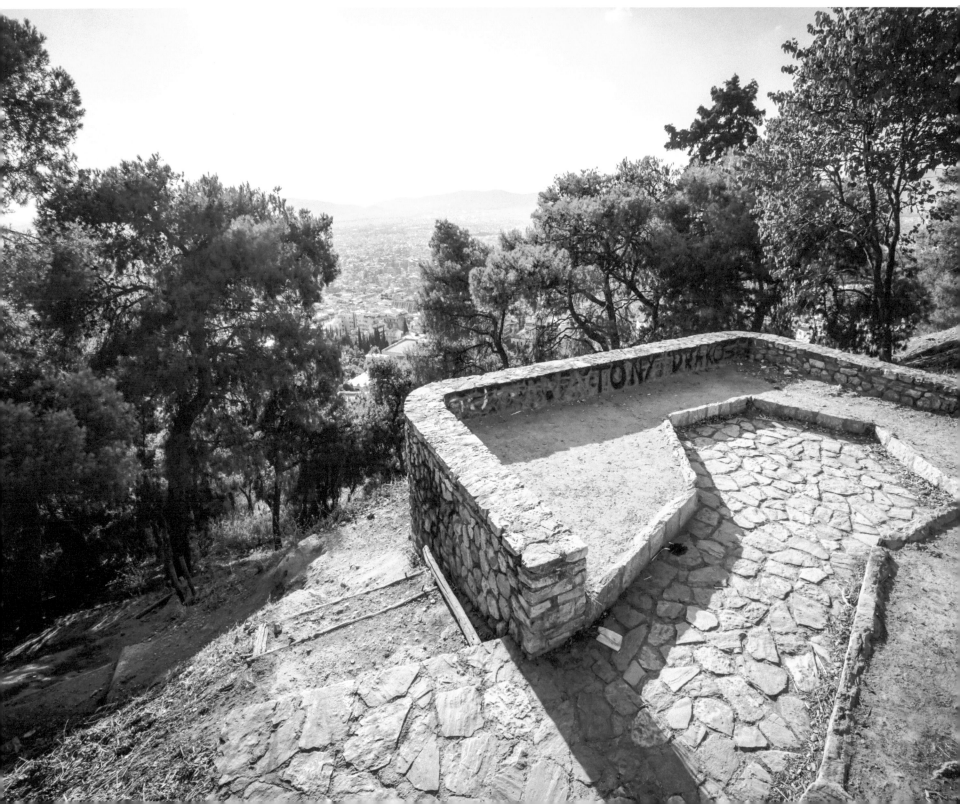

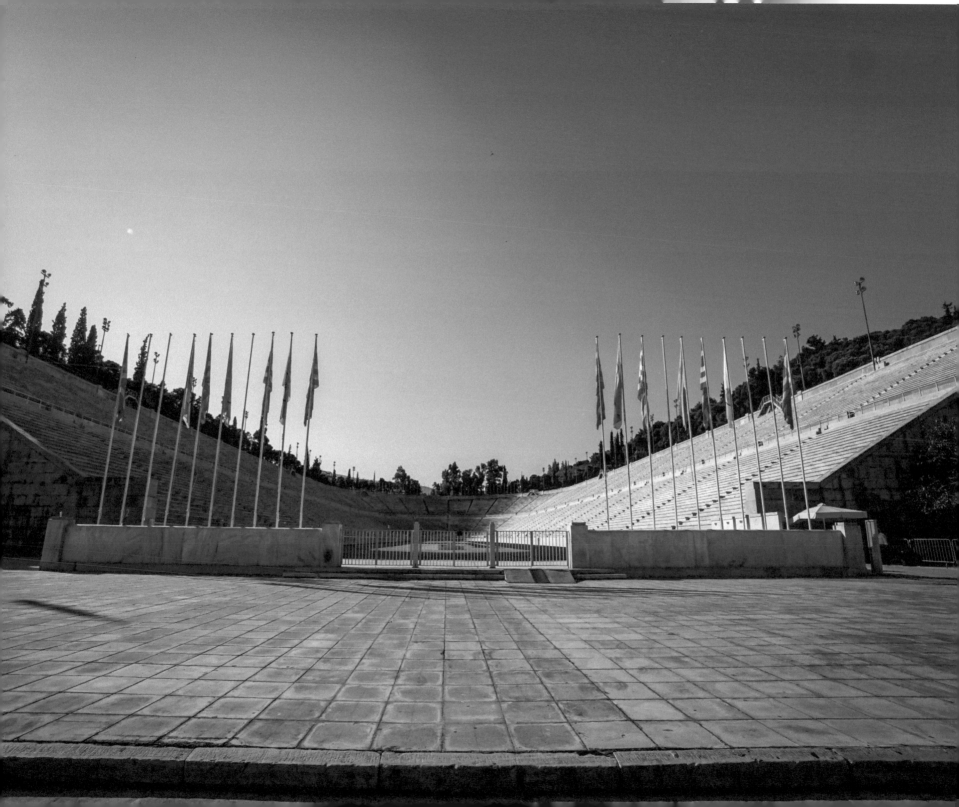

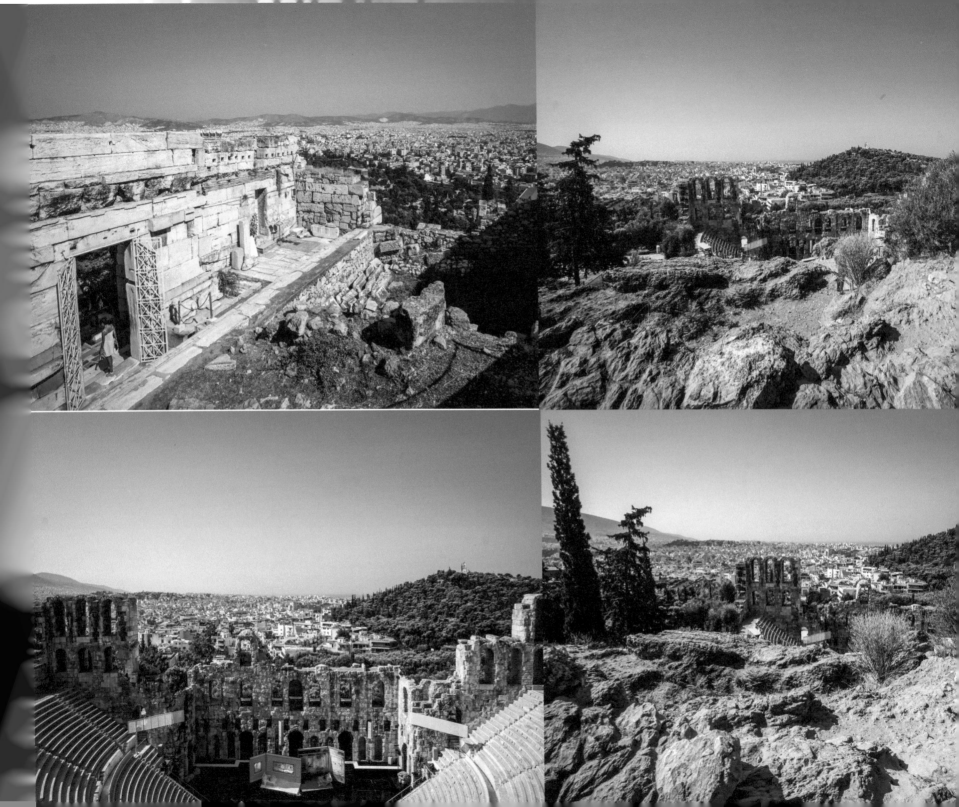

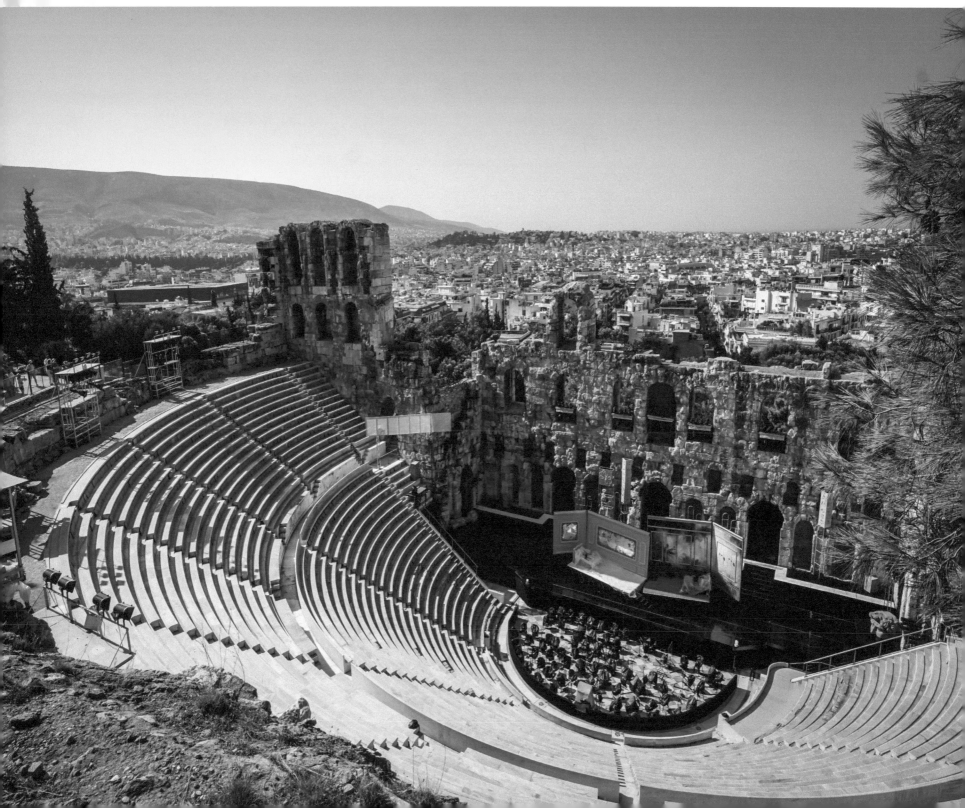

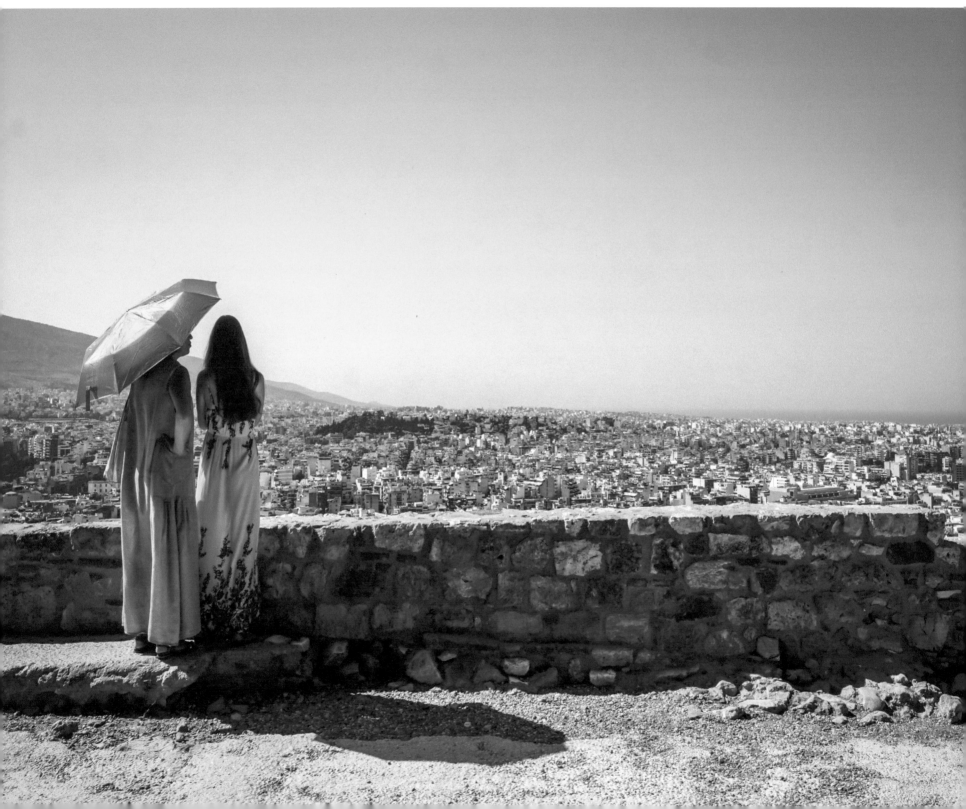

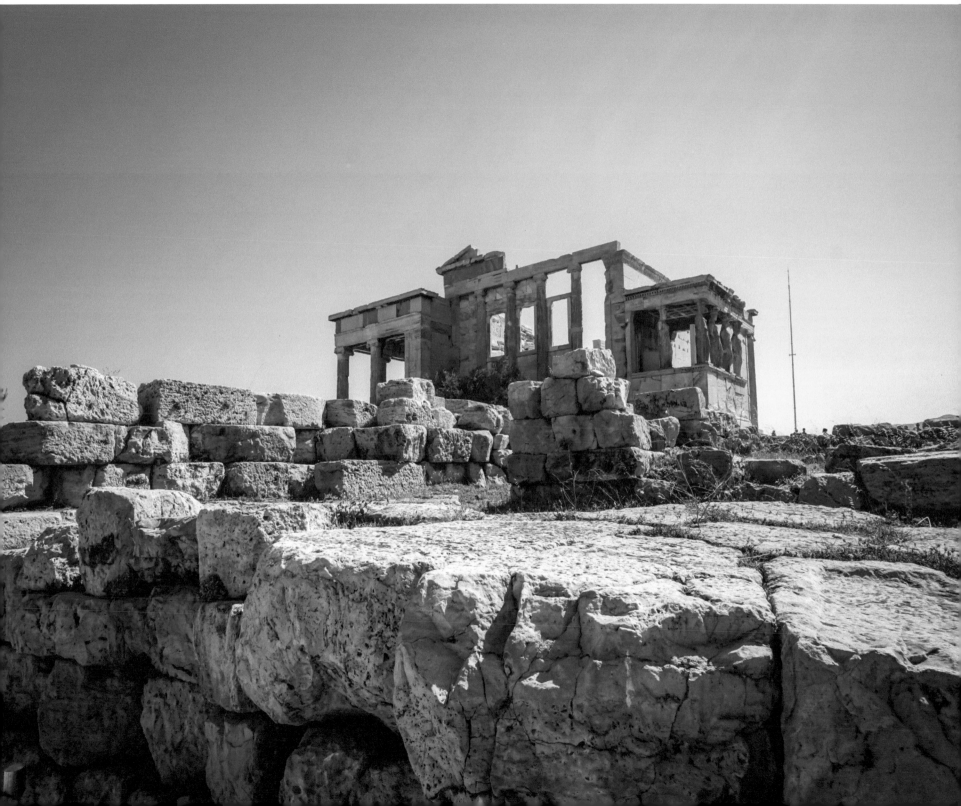

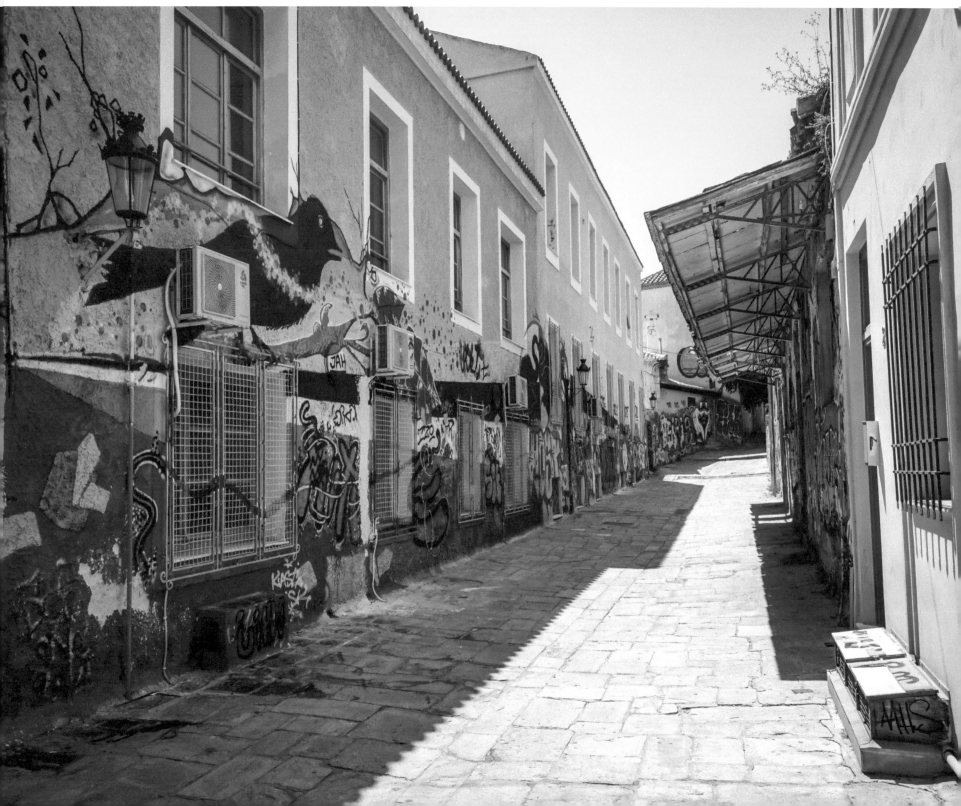

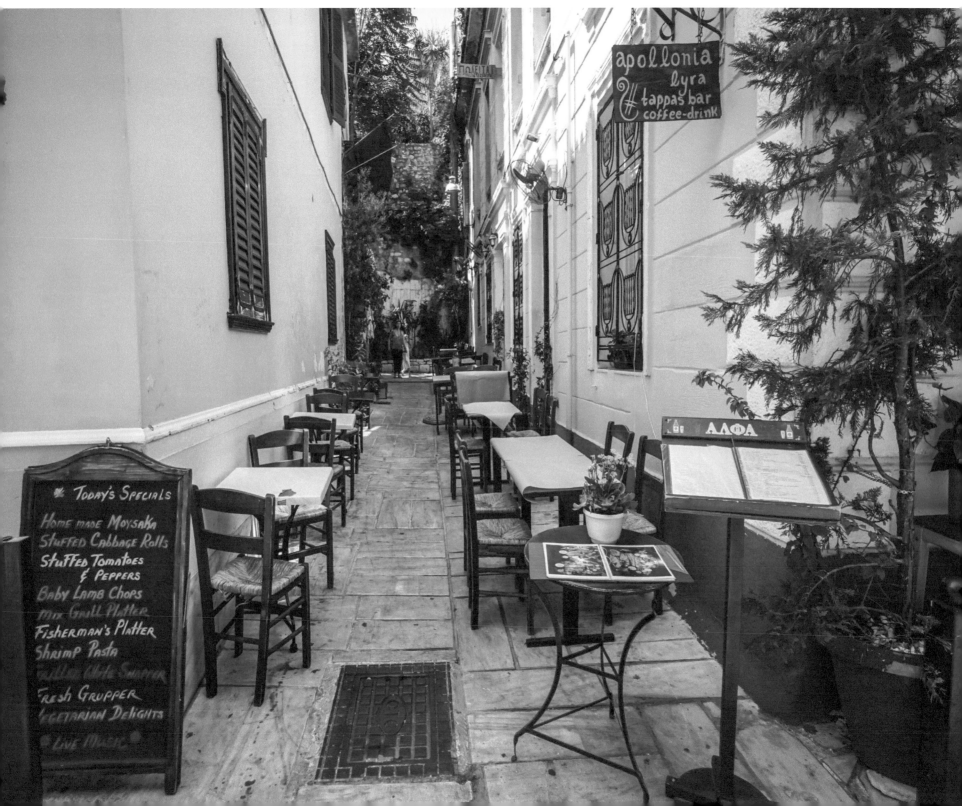

Today's Specials

Home made Moysaka
Stuffed Cabbage Rolls
Stuffed Tomatoes
& Peppers
Baby Lamb Chops
Mix Grill Platter
Fisherman's Platter
Shrimp Pasta
Grilled White Snapper
Fresh Grupper
Vegetarian Delights
• Live Music •

apollonia
lyra
tappas bar
coffee-drink

ΑΛΦΑ

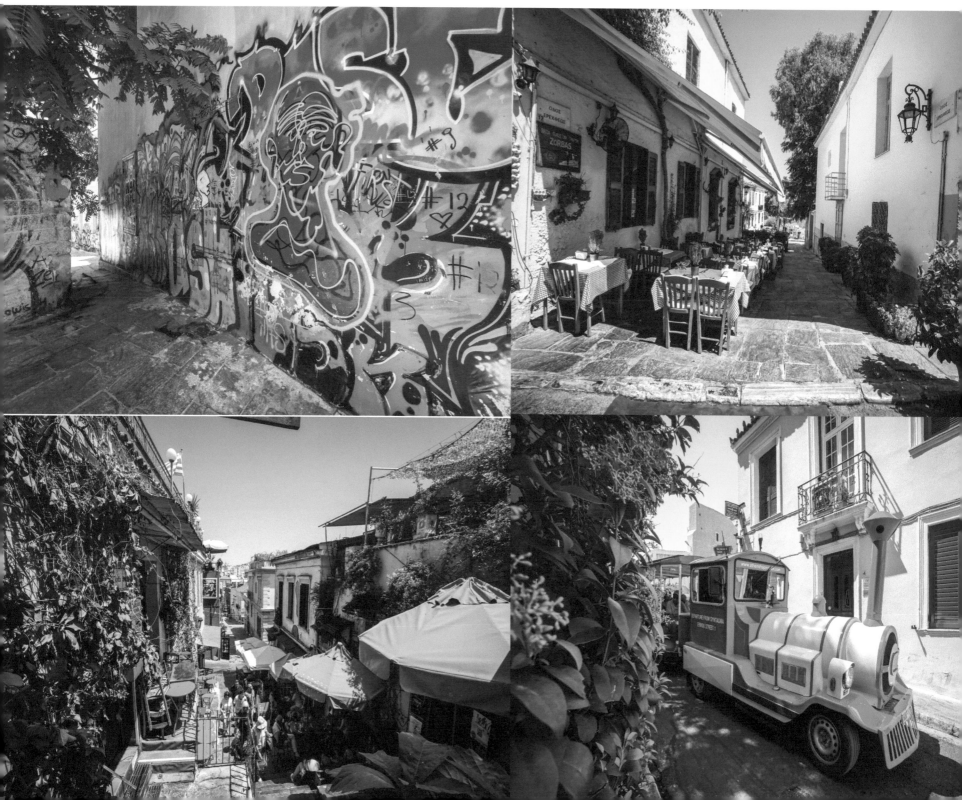

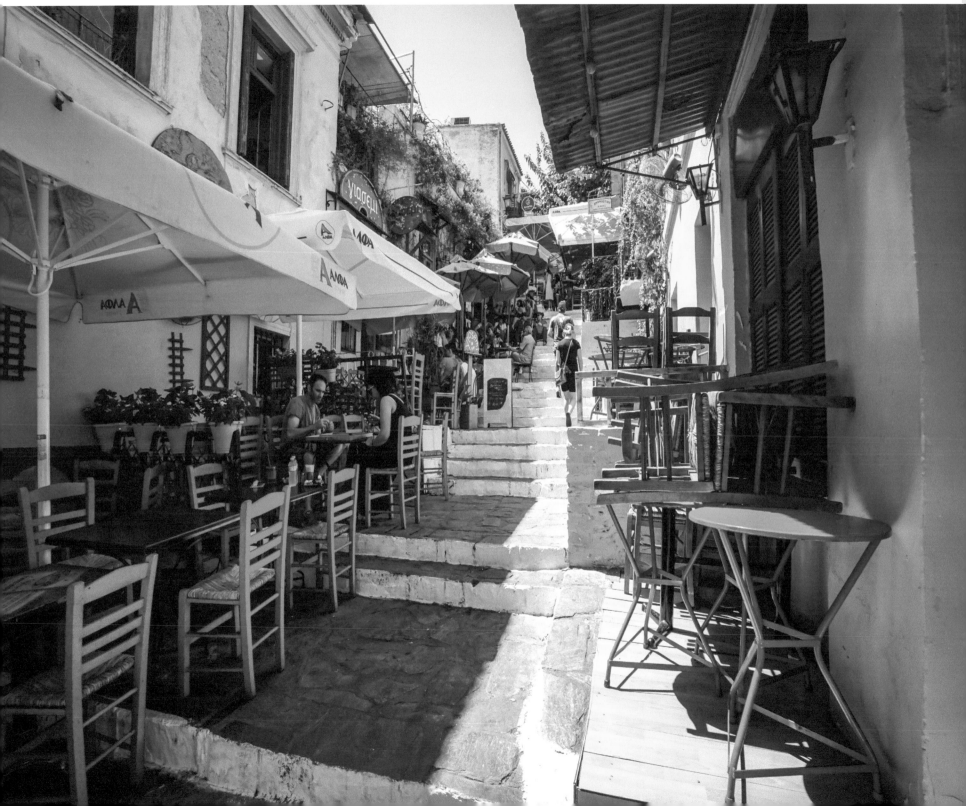

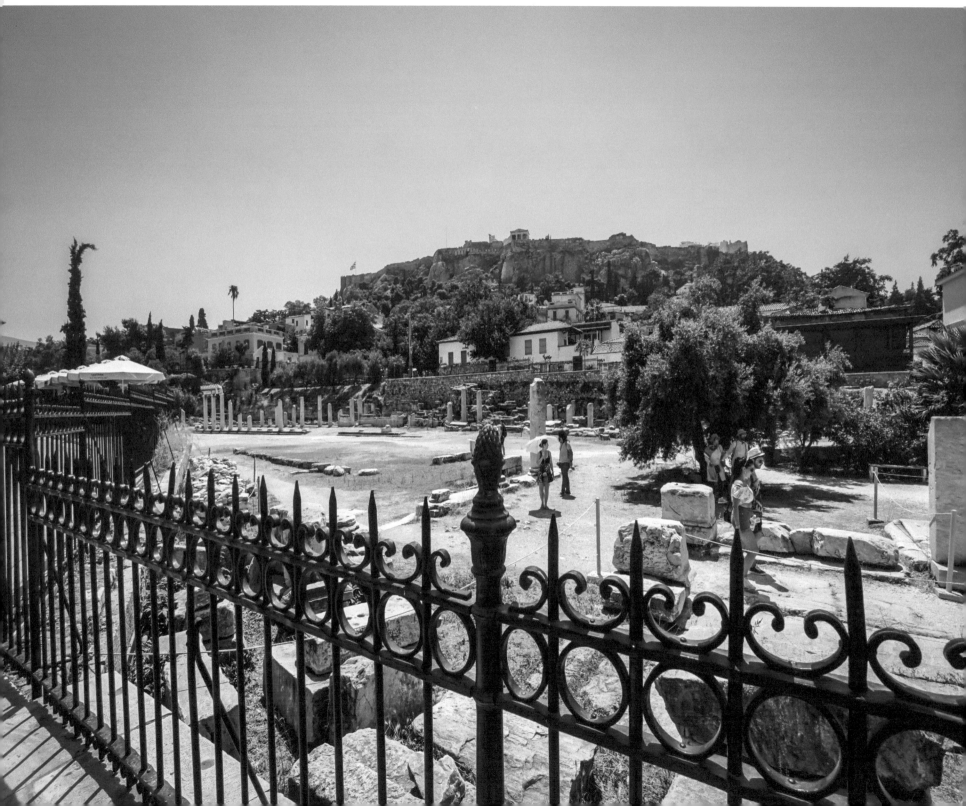

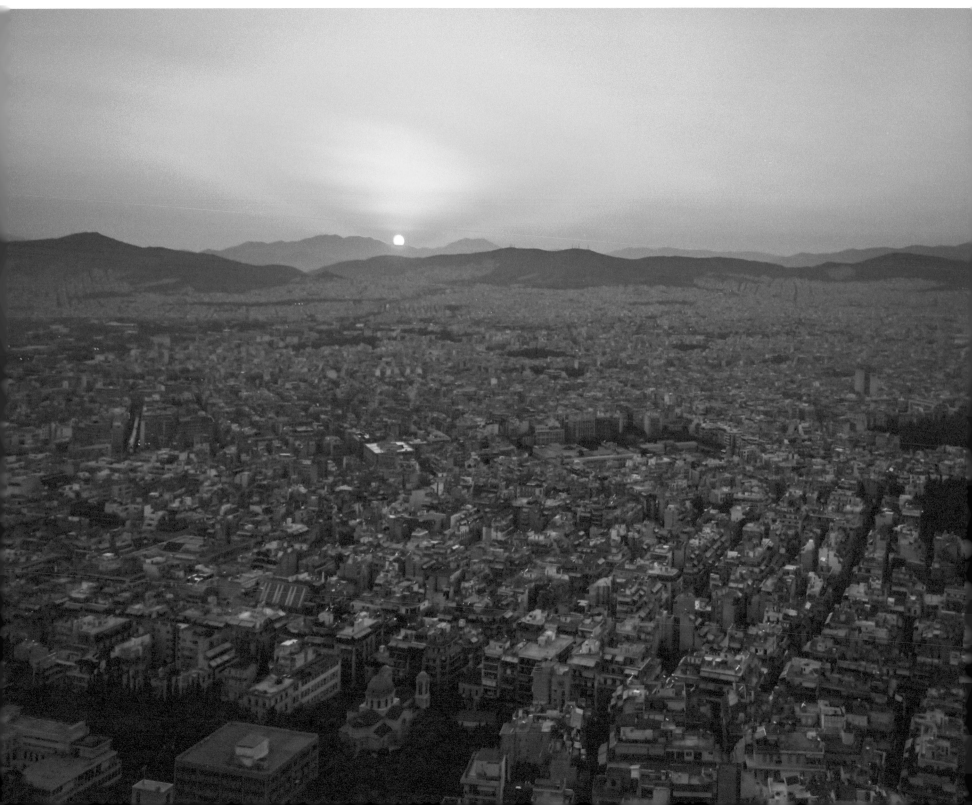

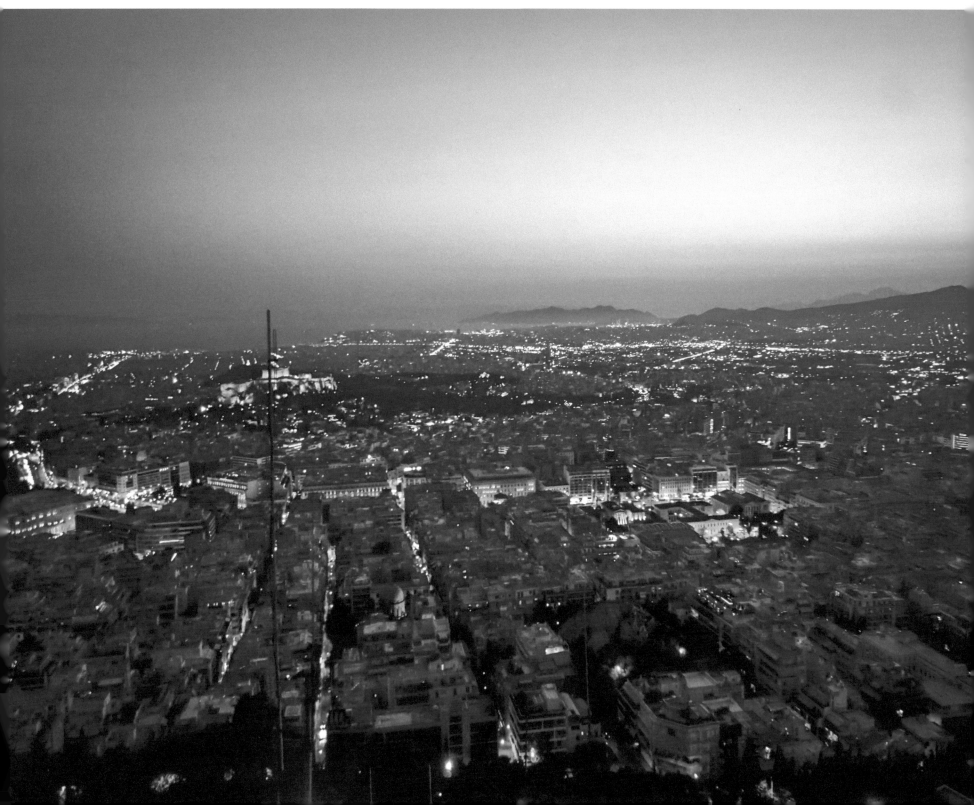

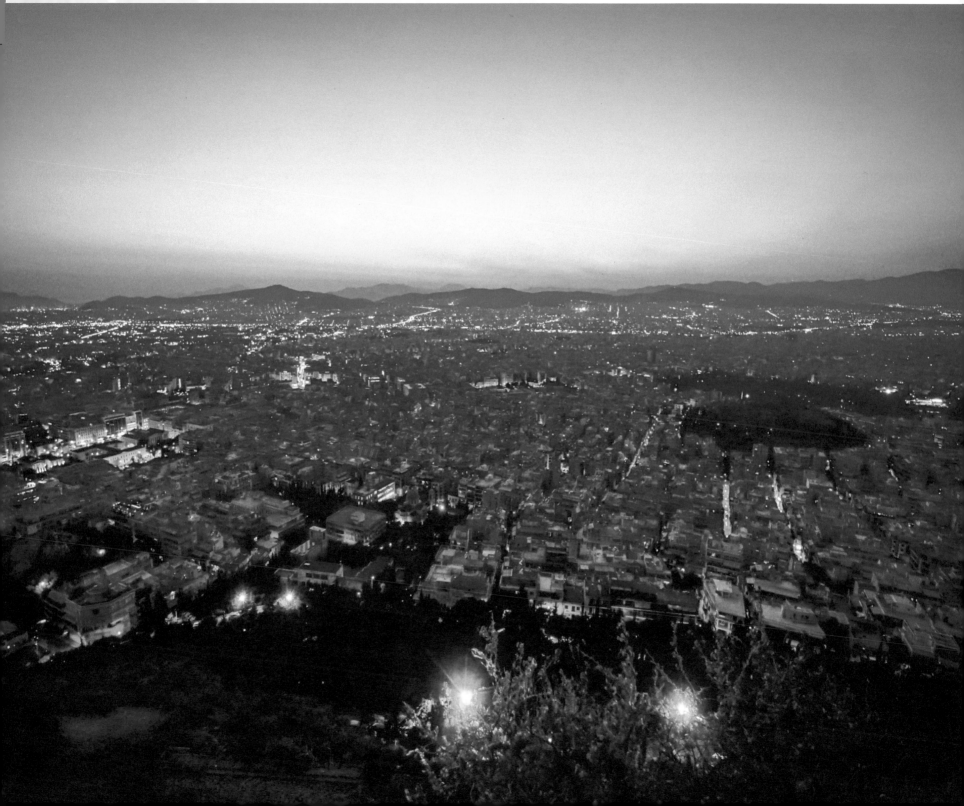

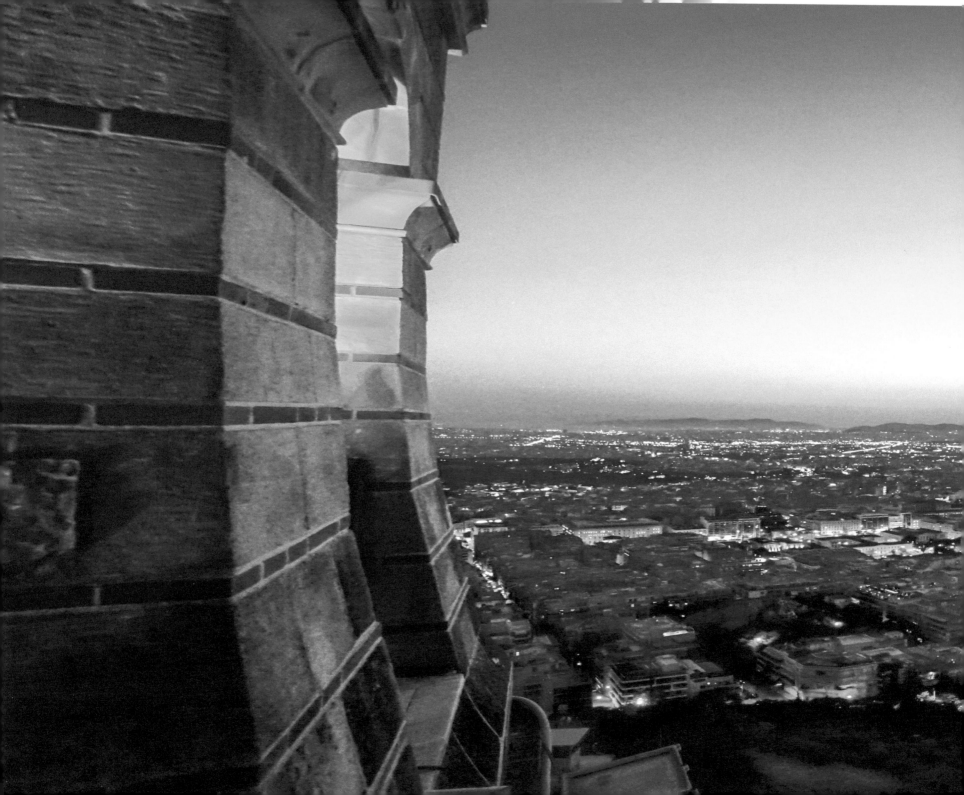

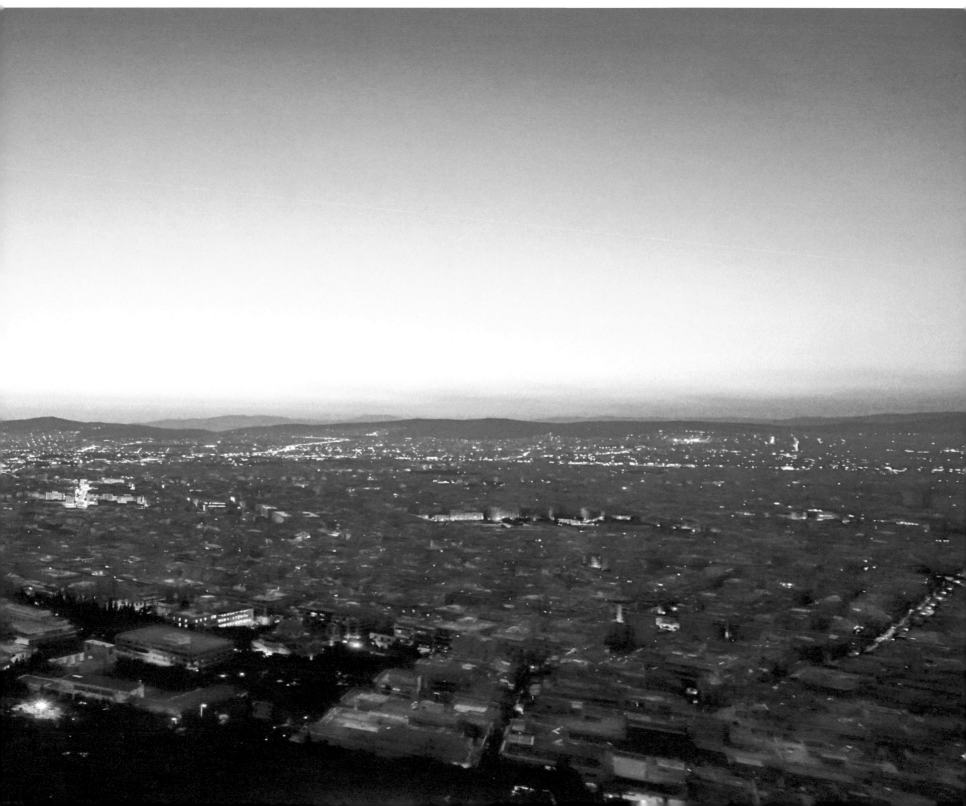

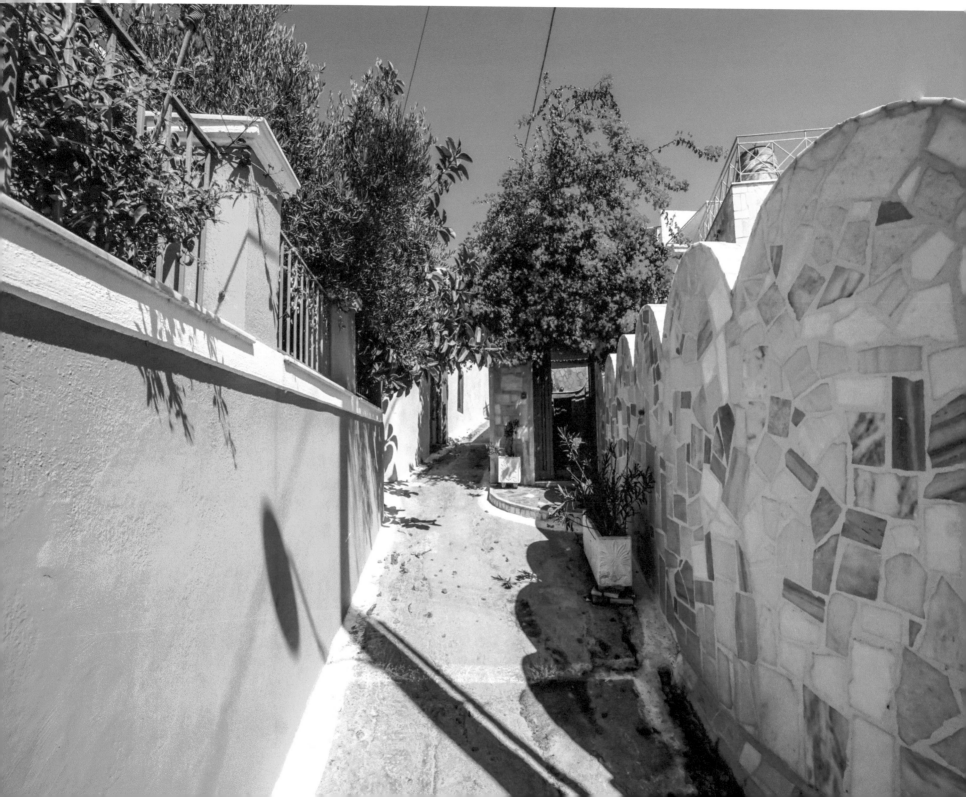

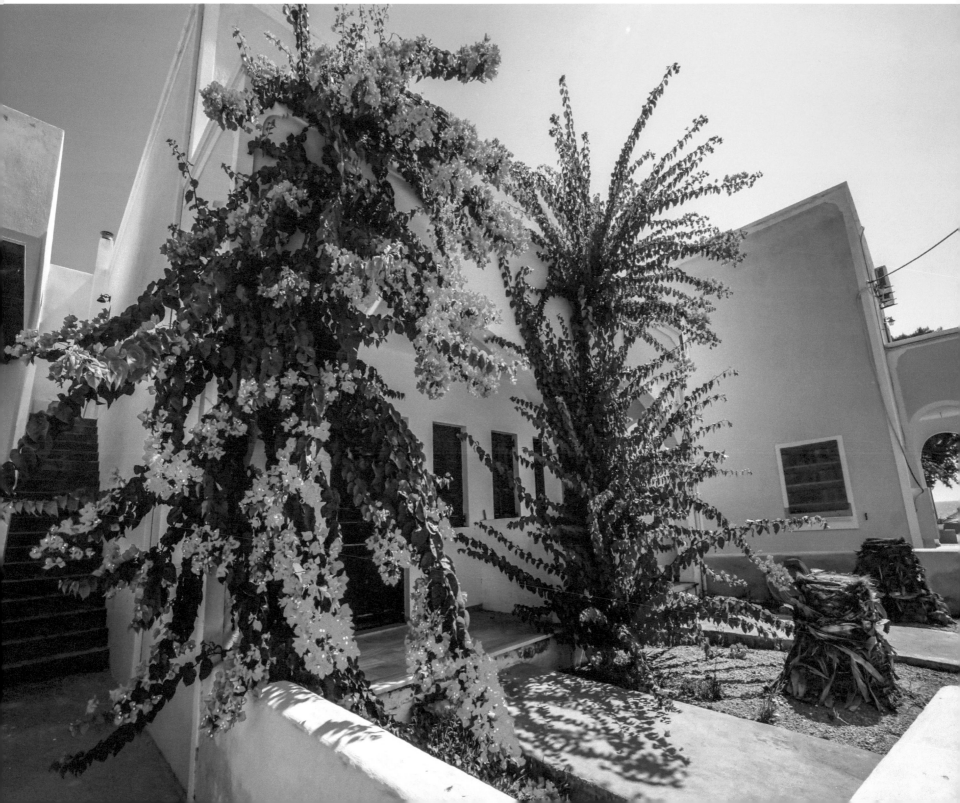

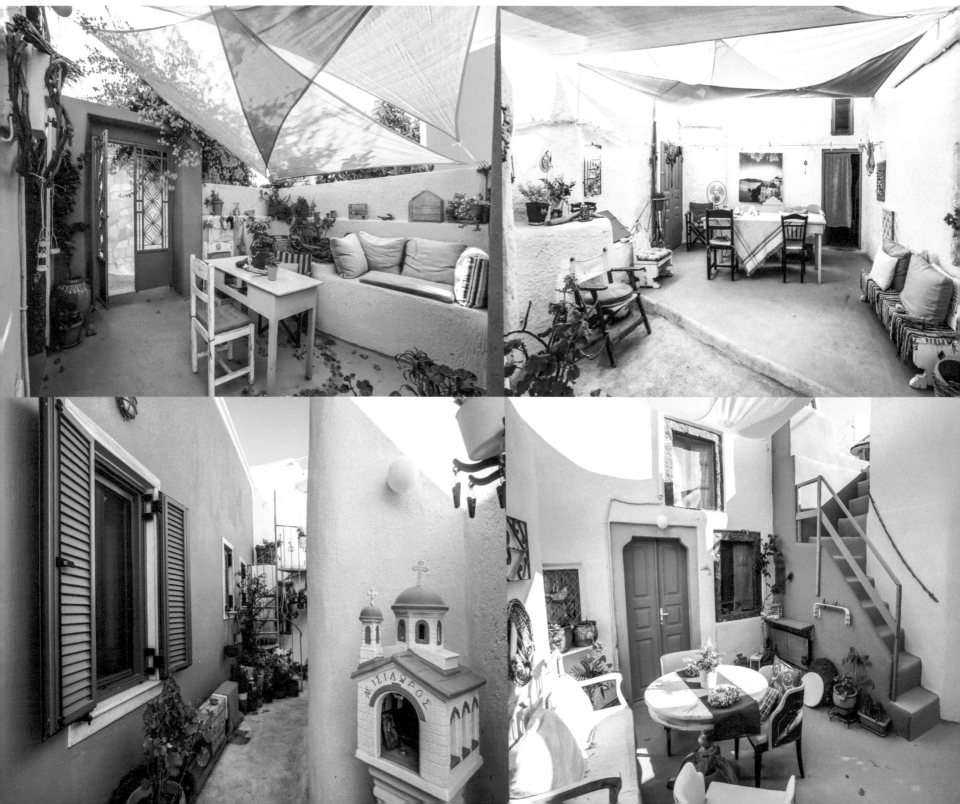

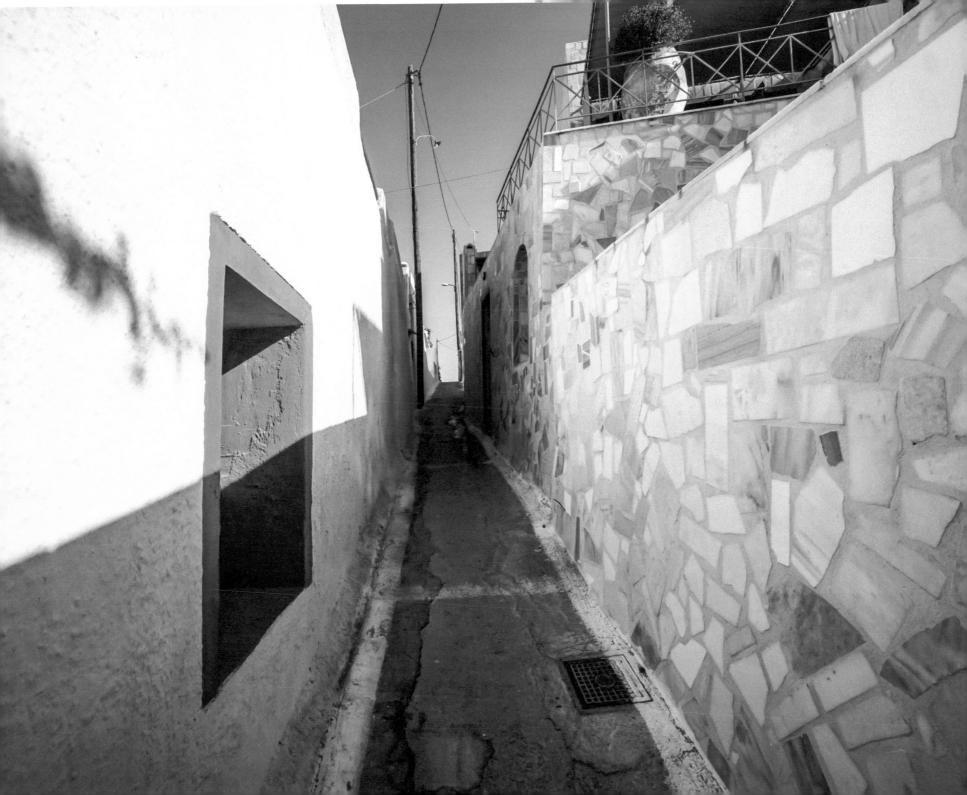

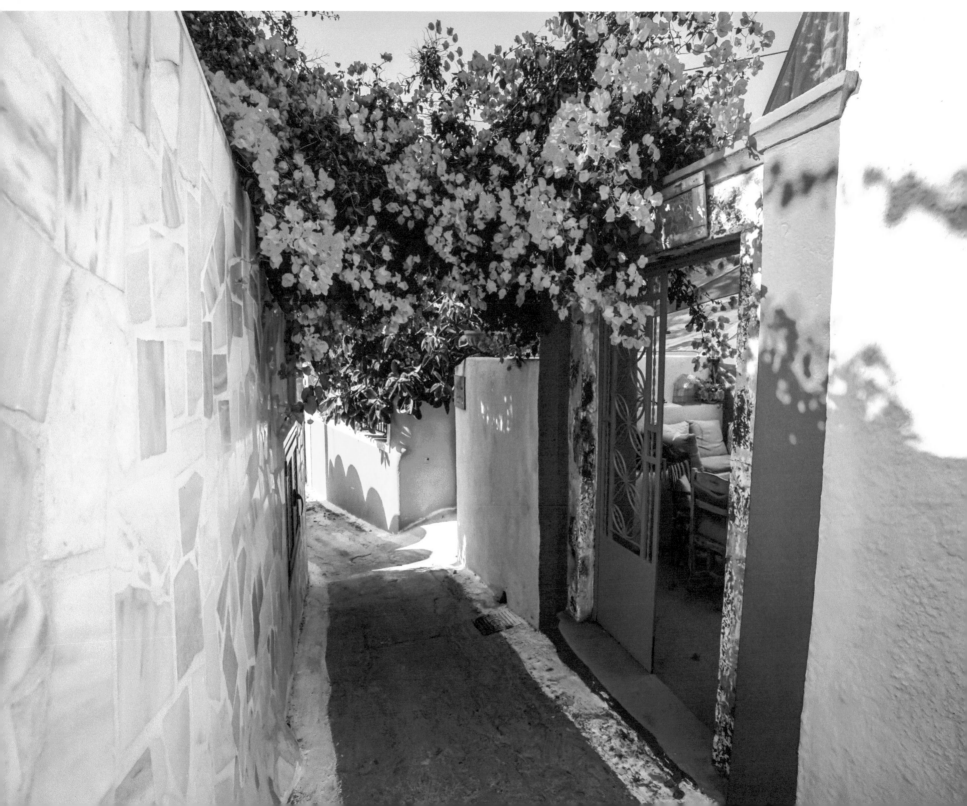

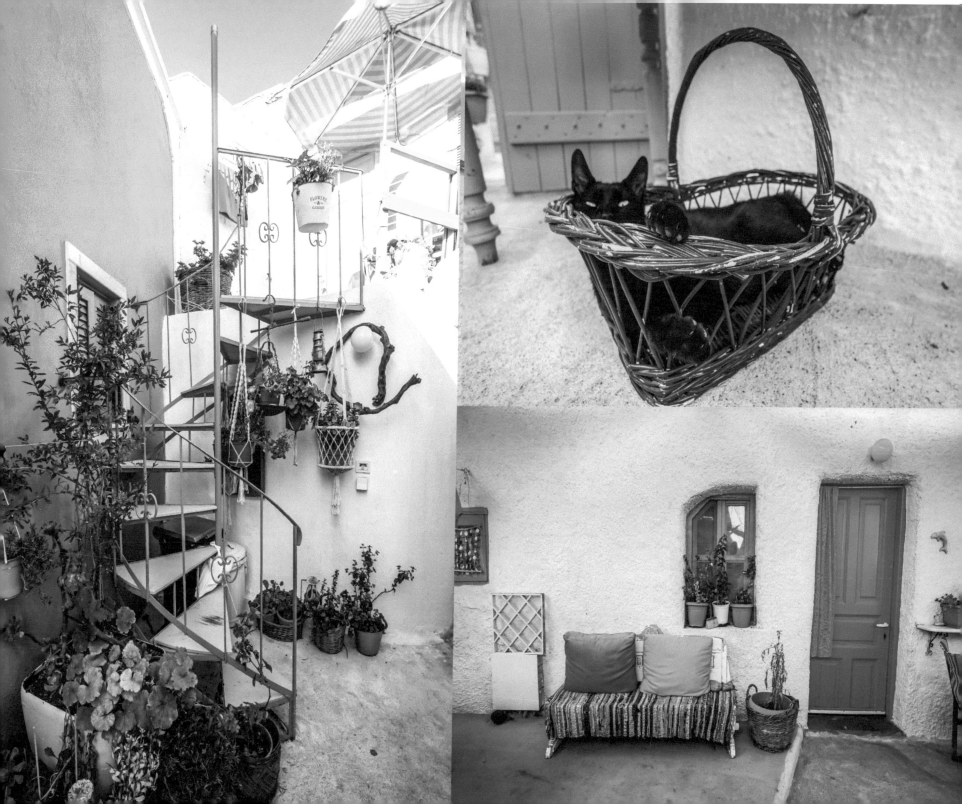

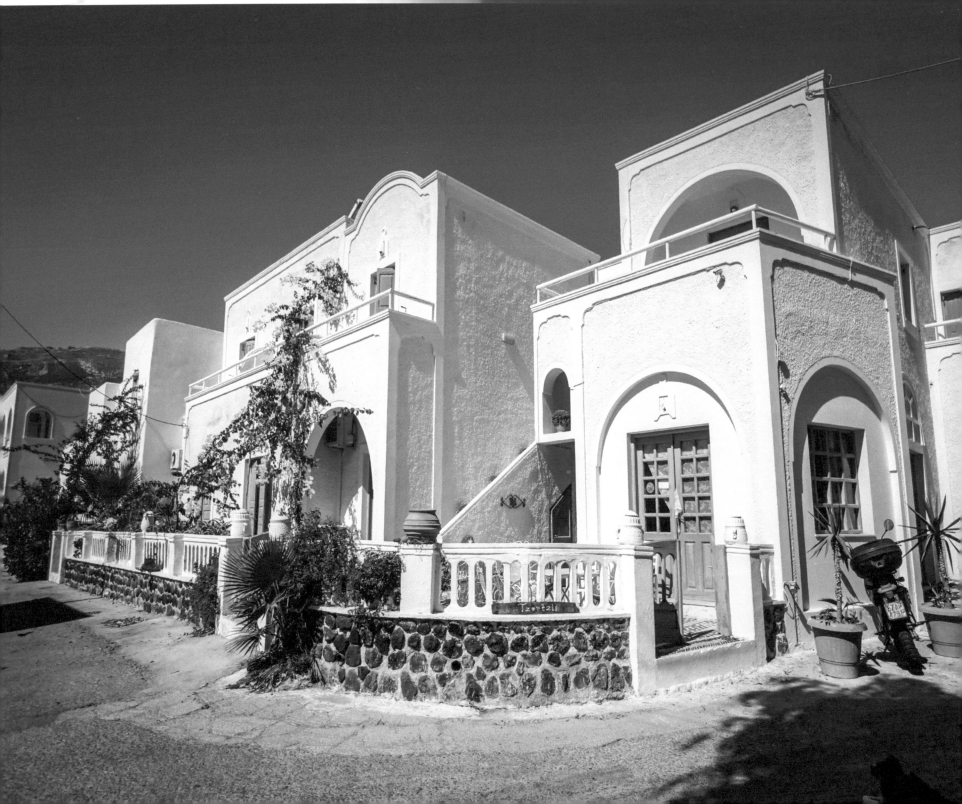

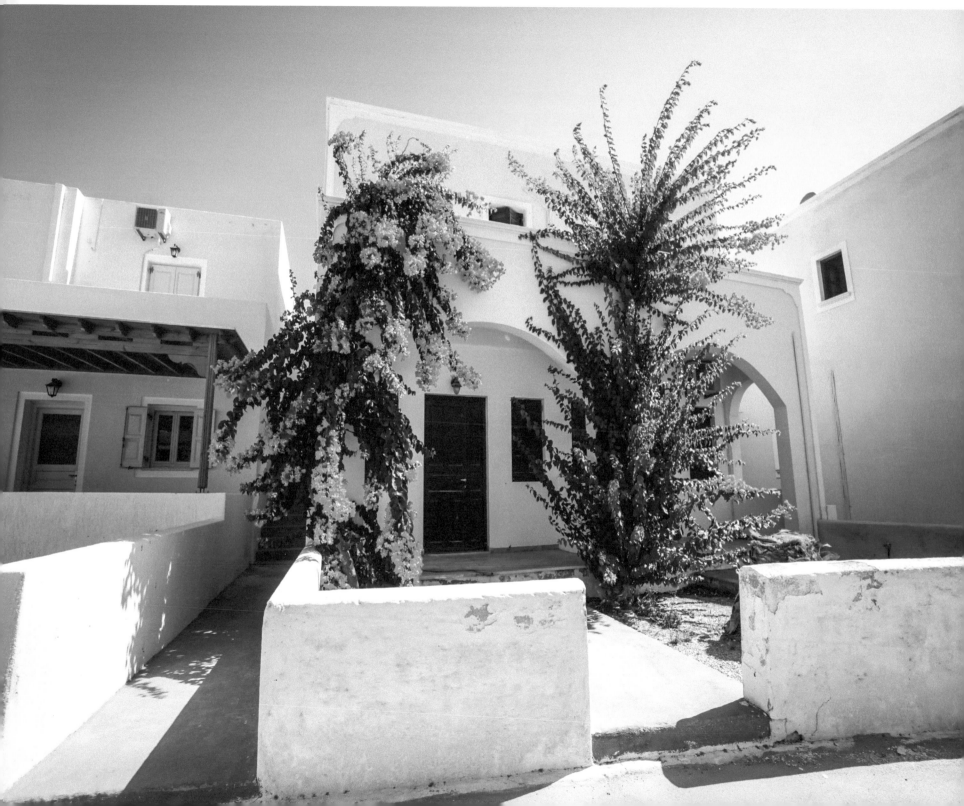

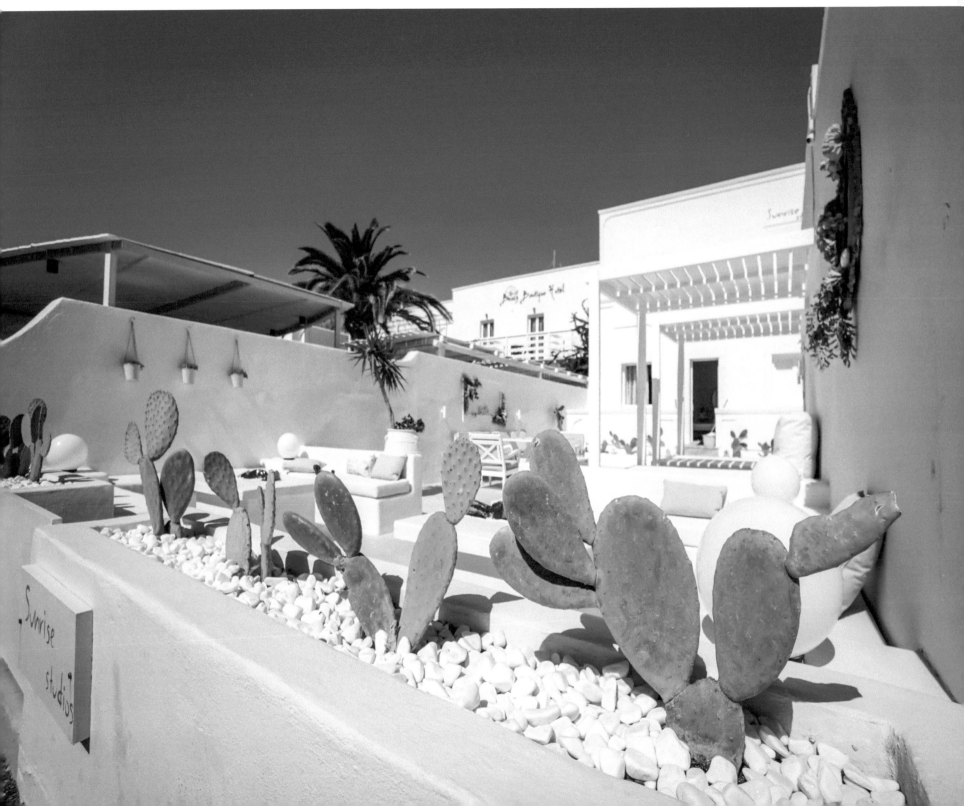

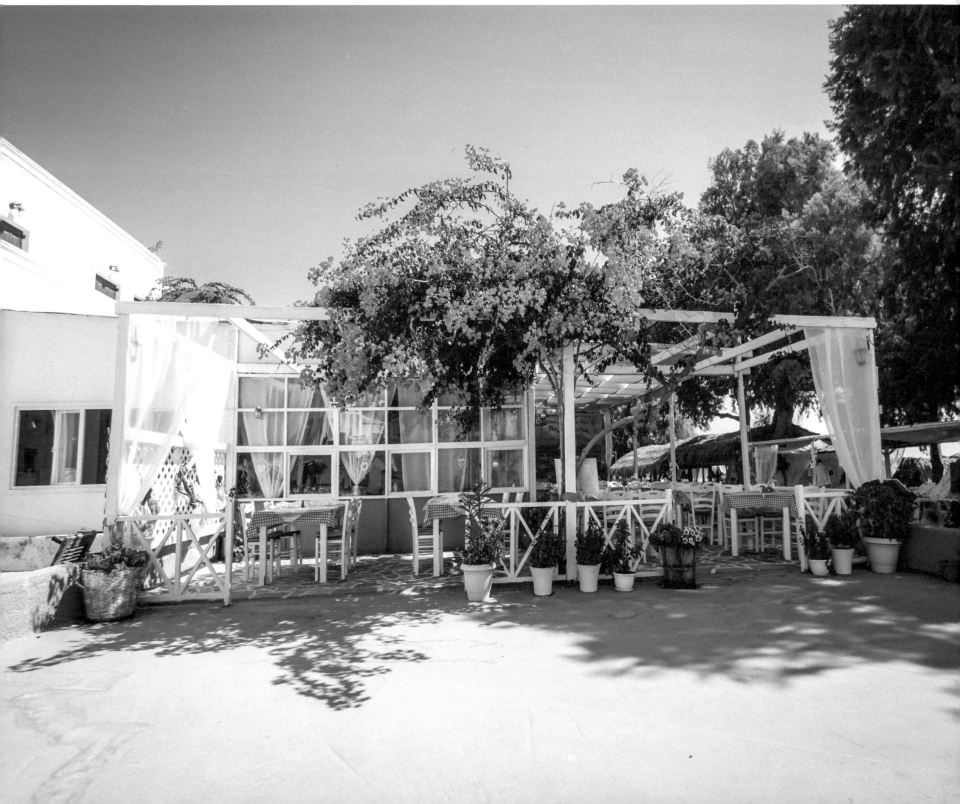

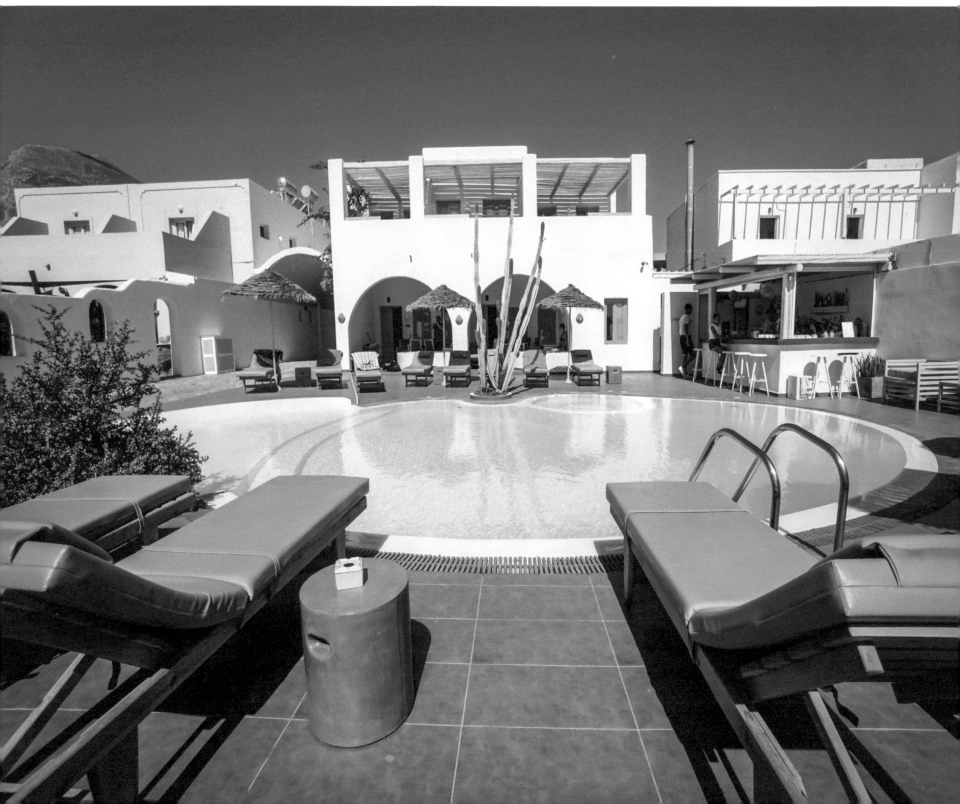

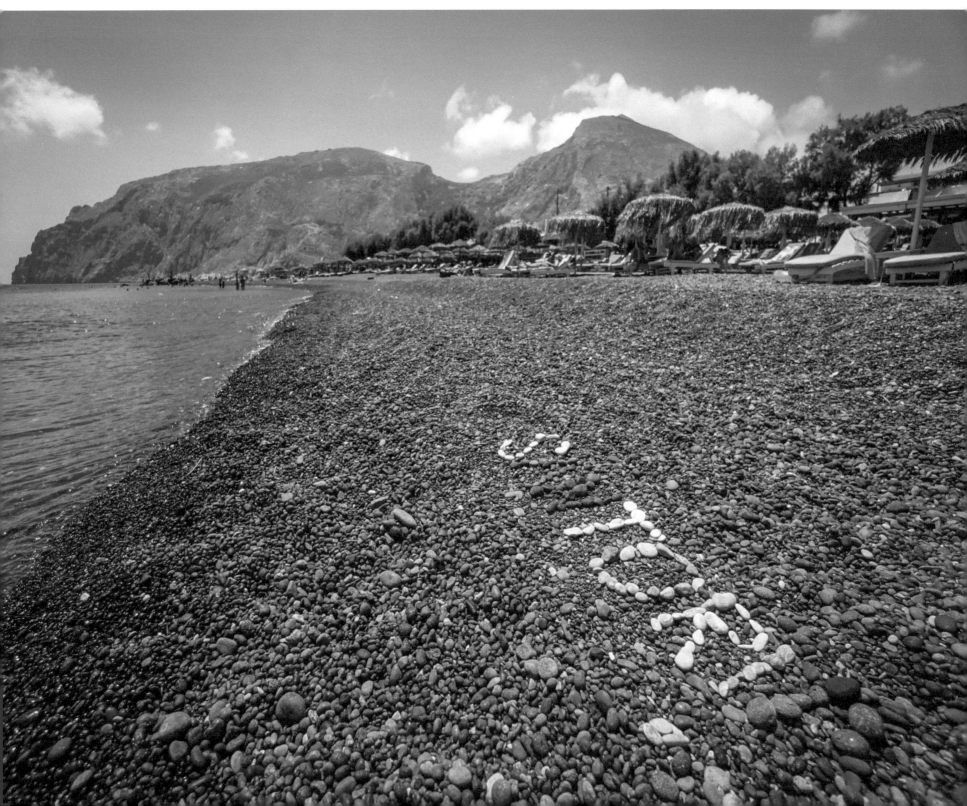

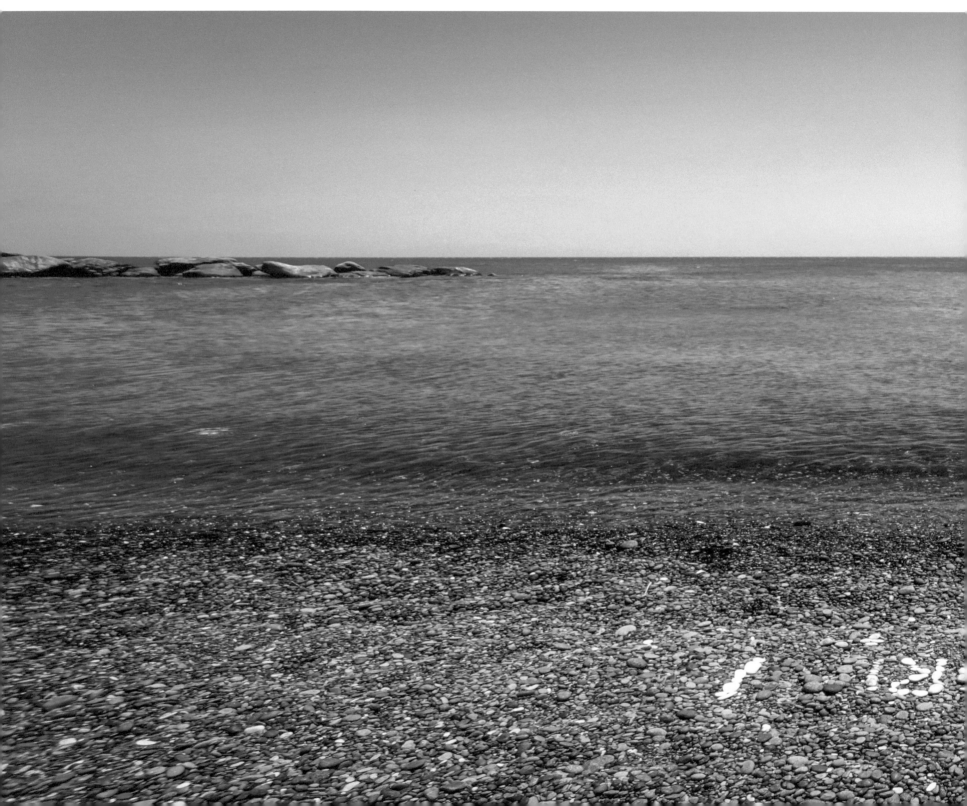

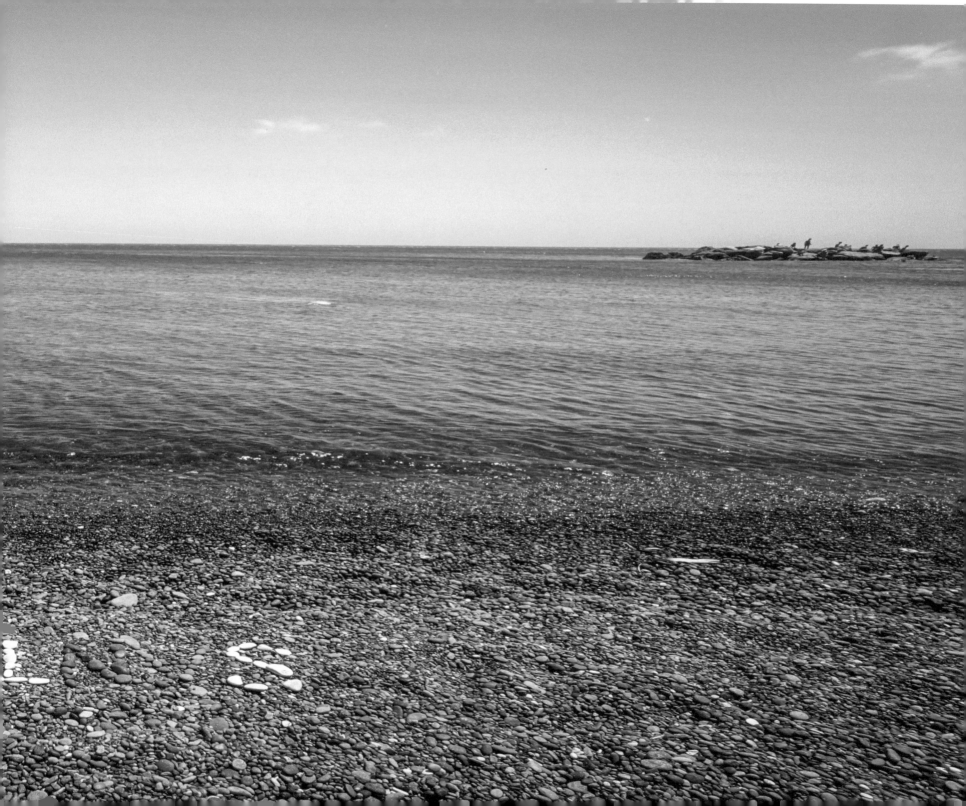

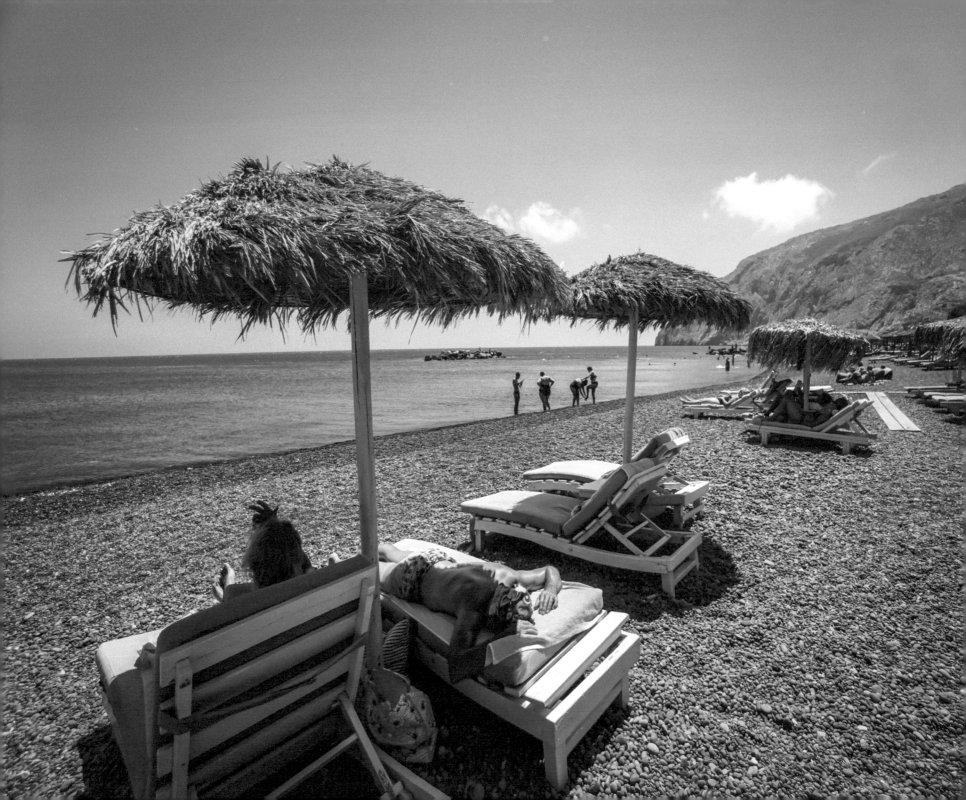

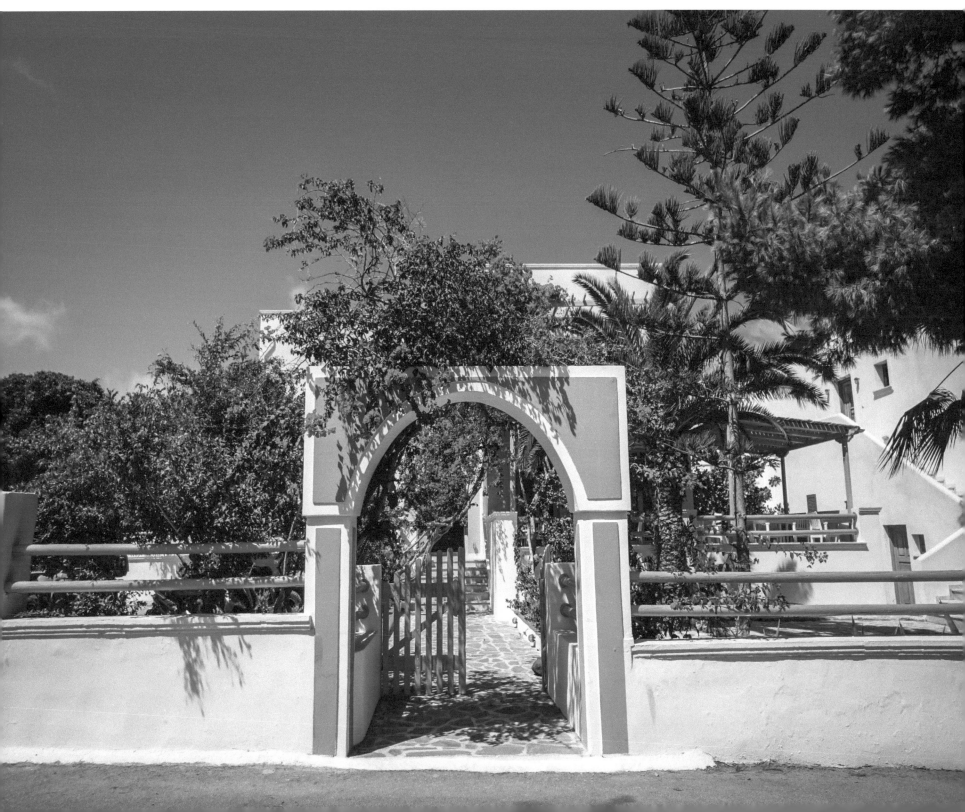

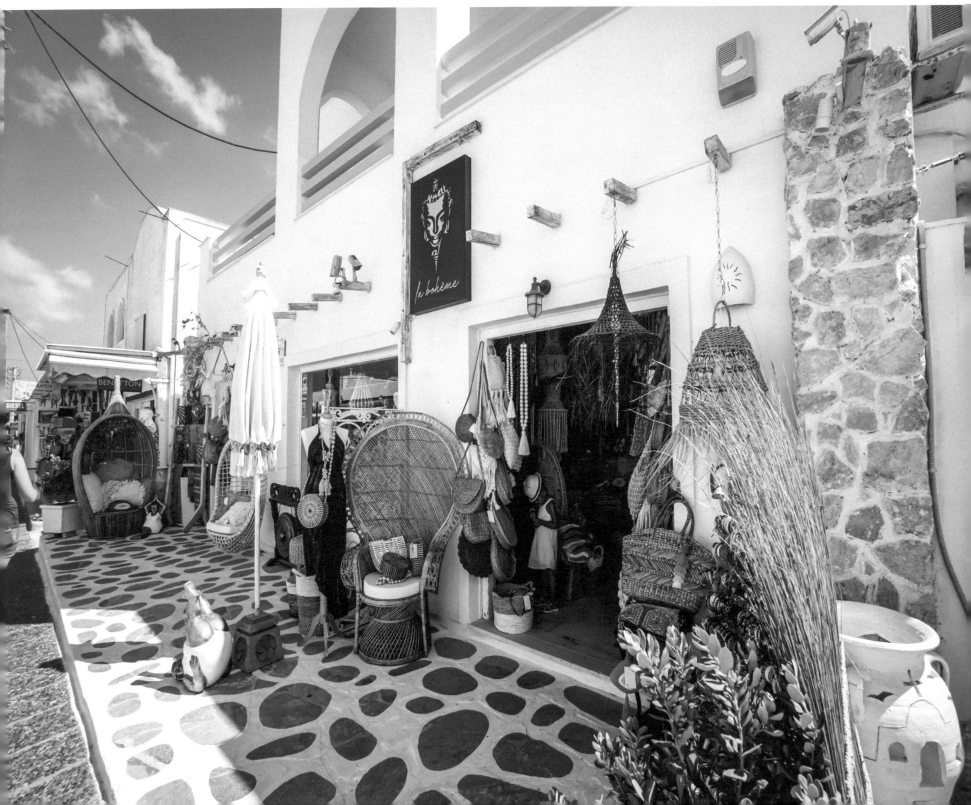

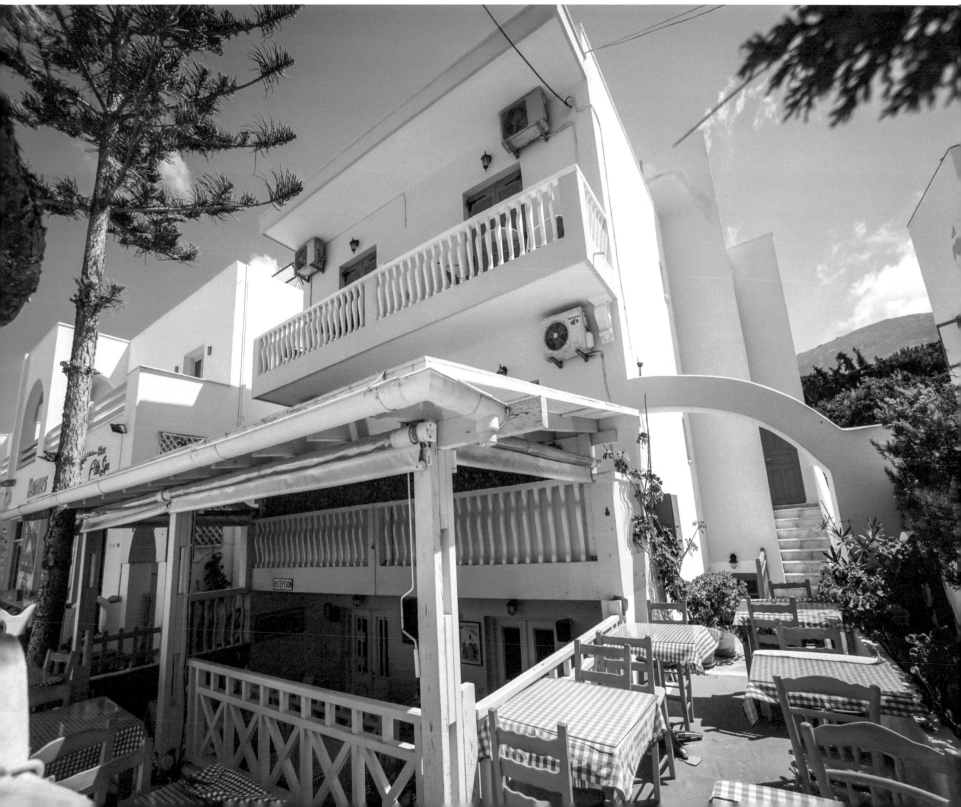

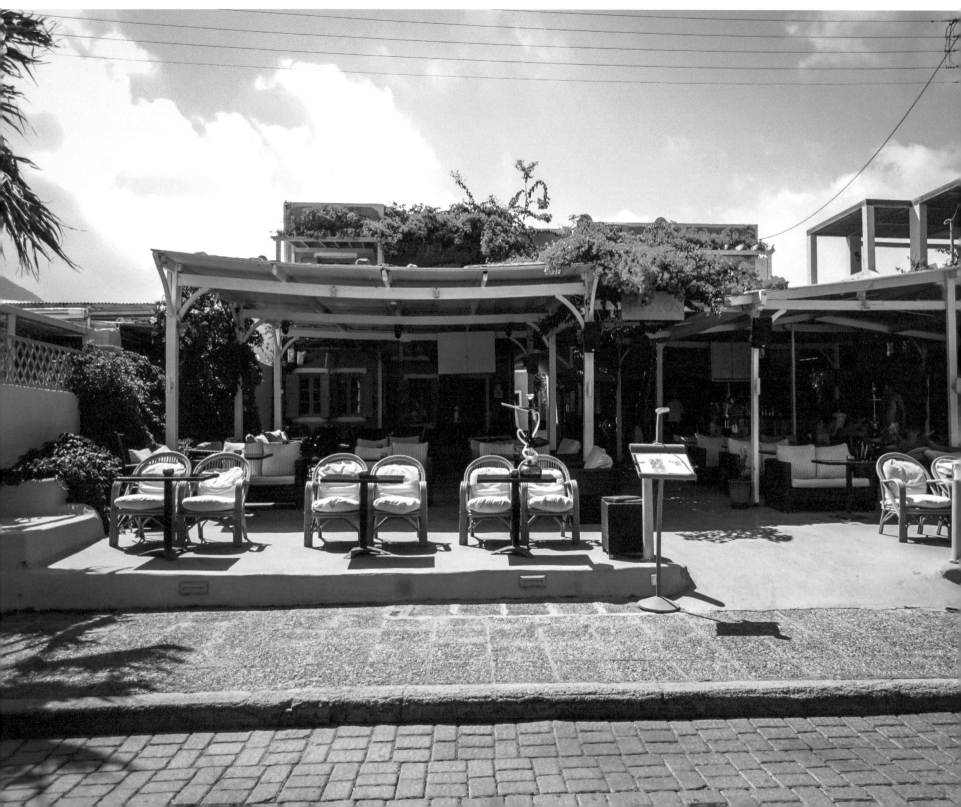

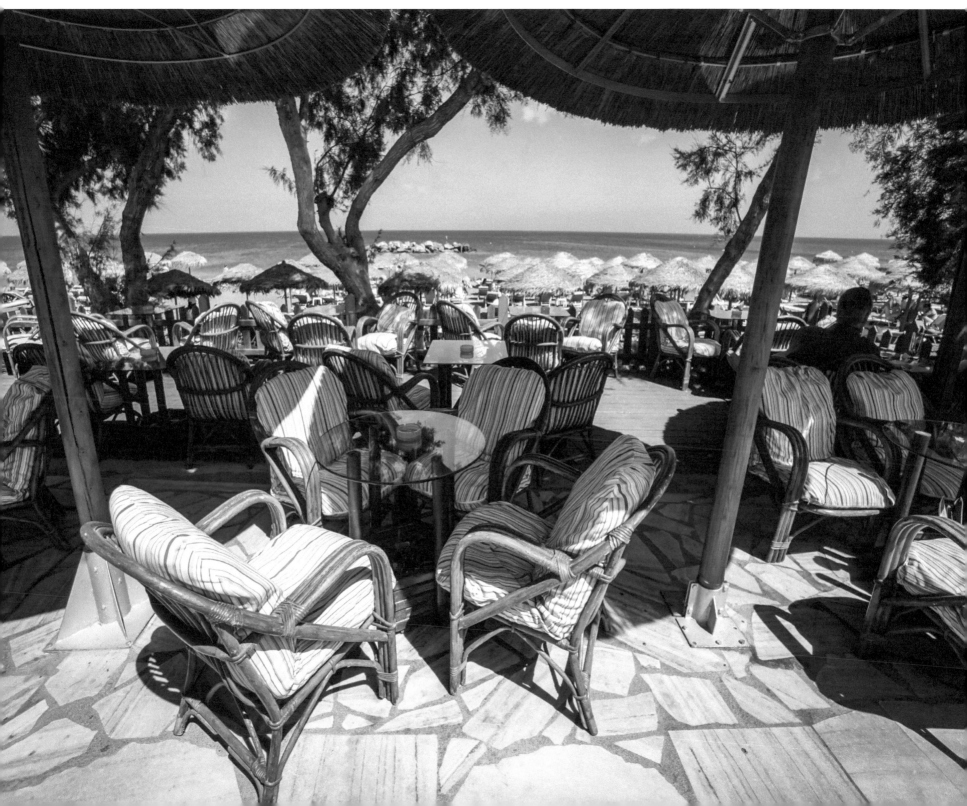

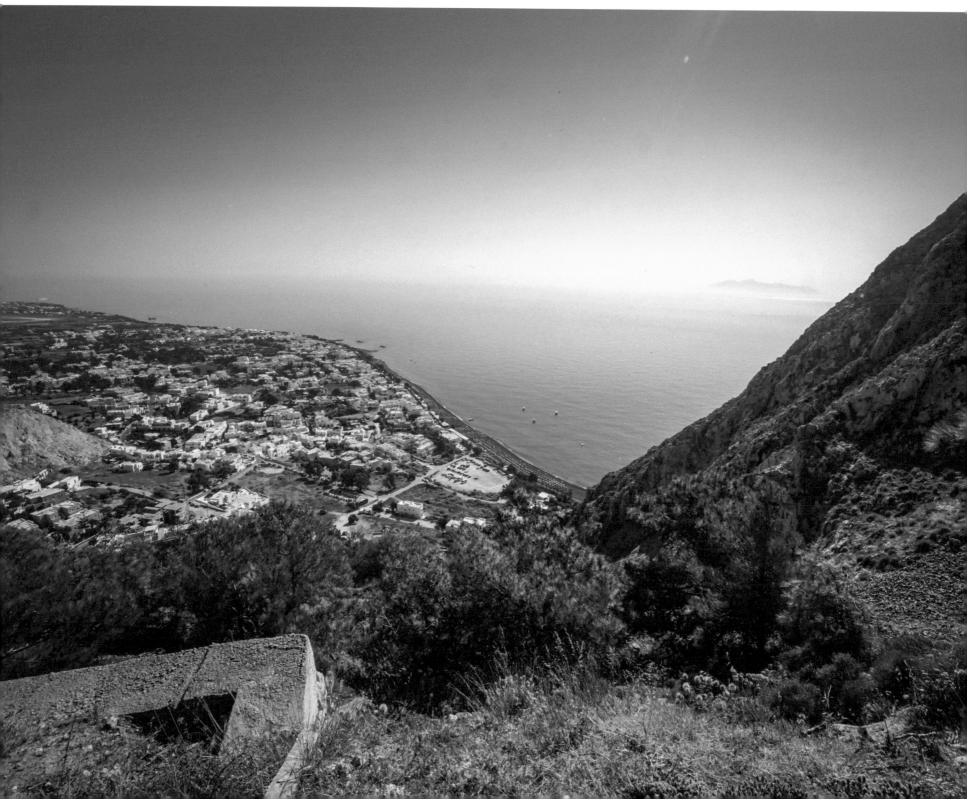

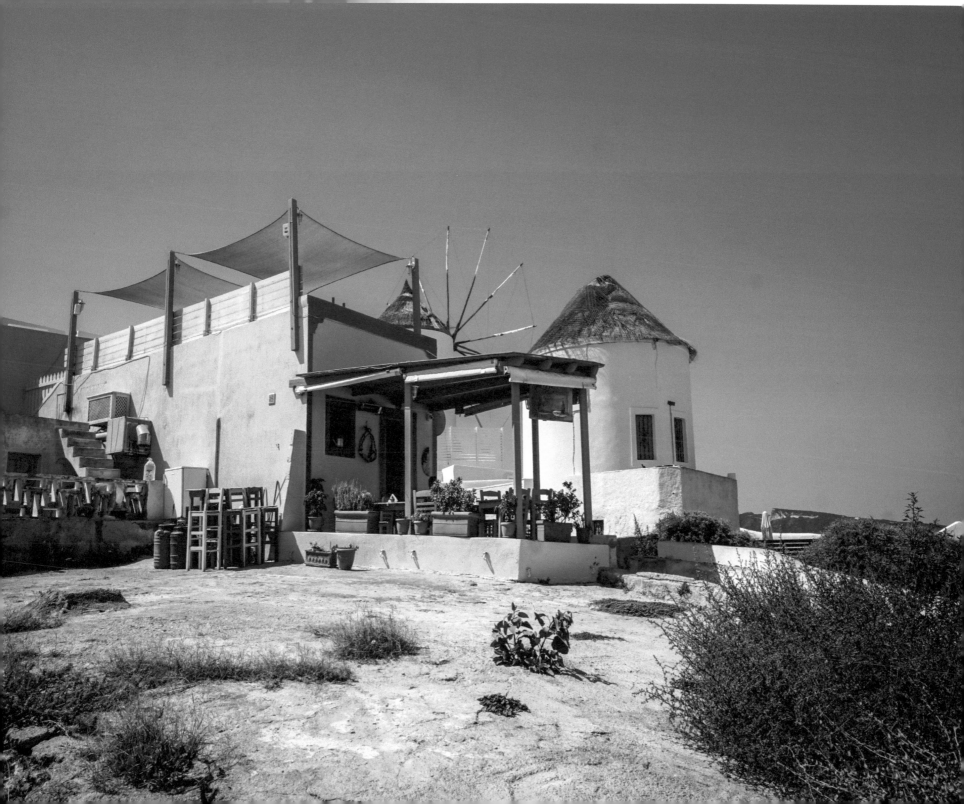

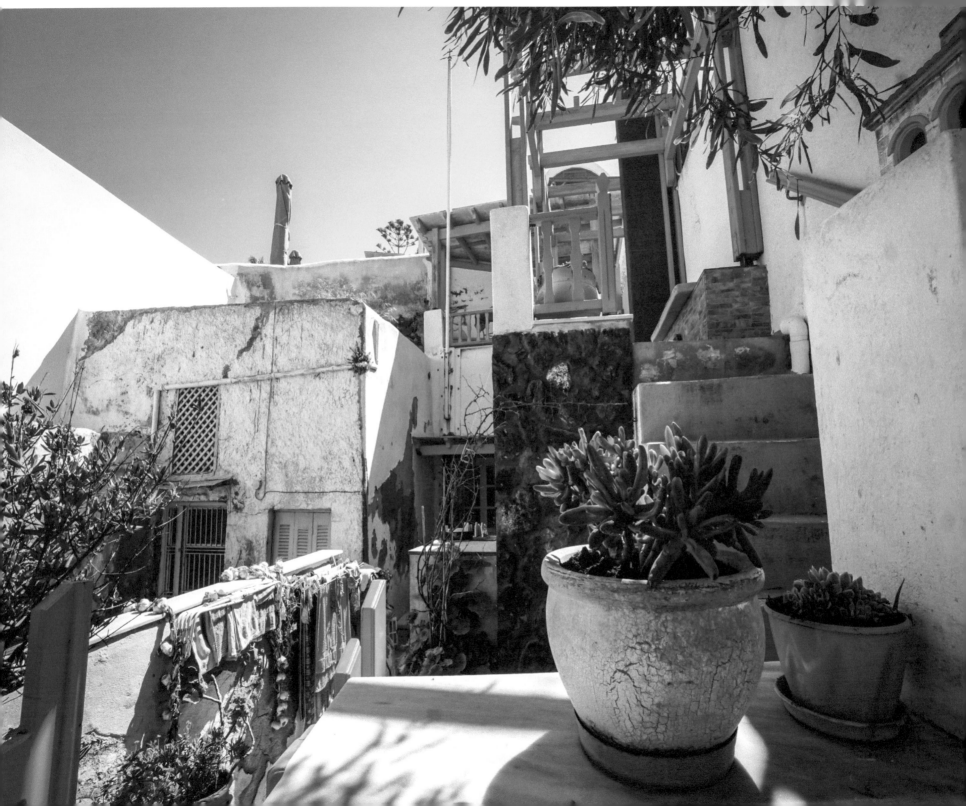

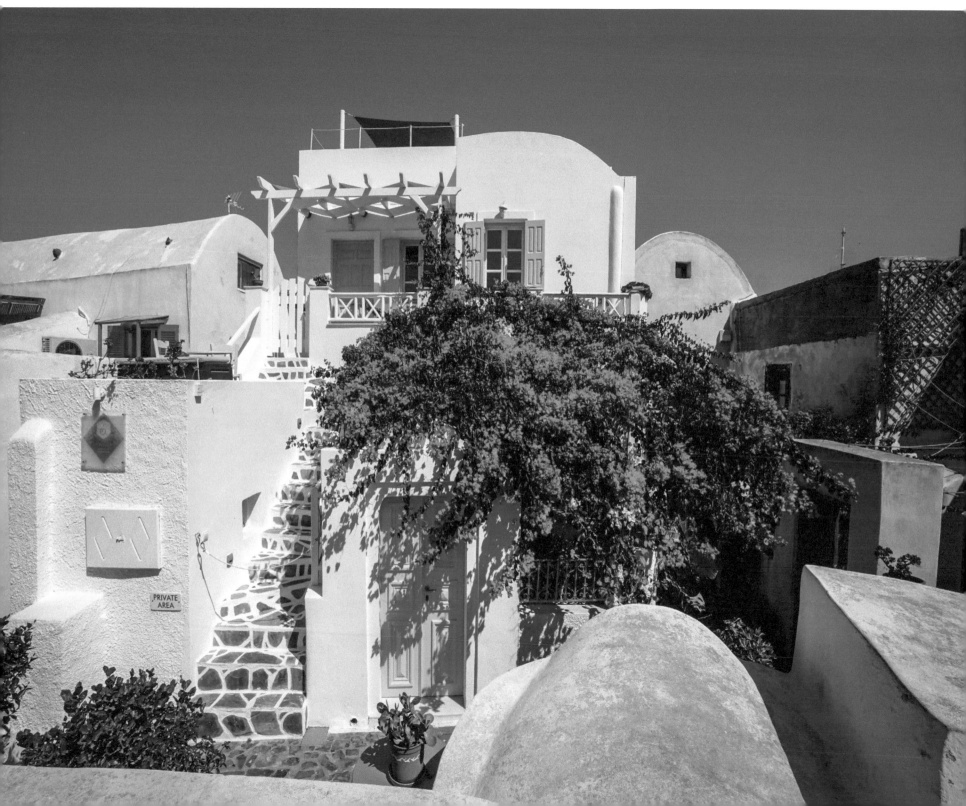

PRIVATE AREA

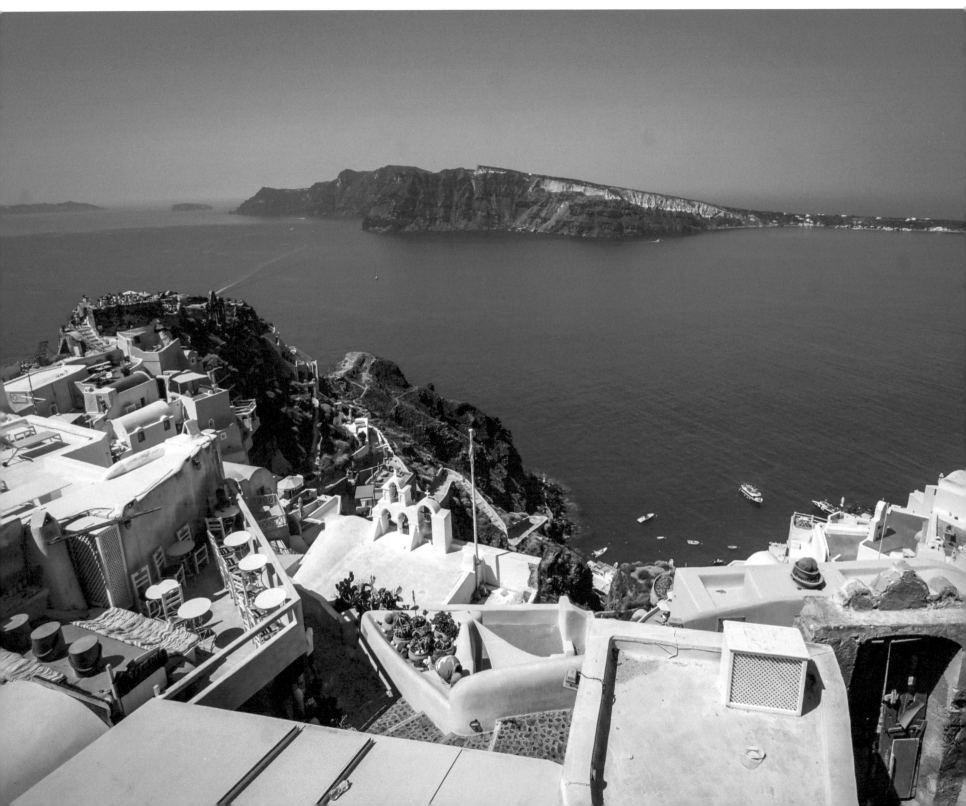

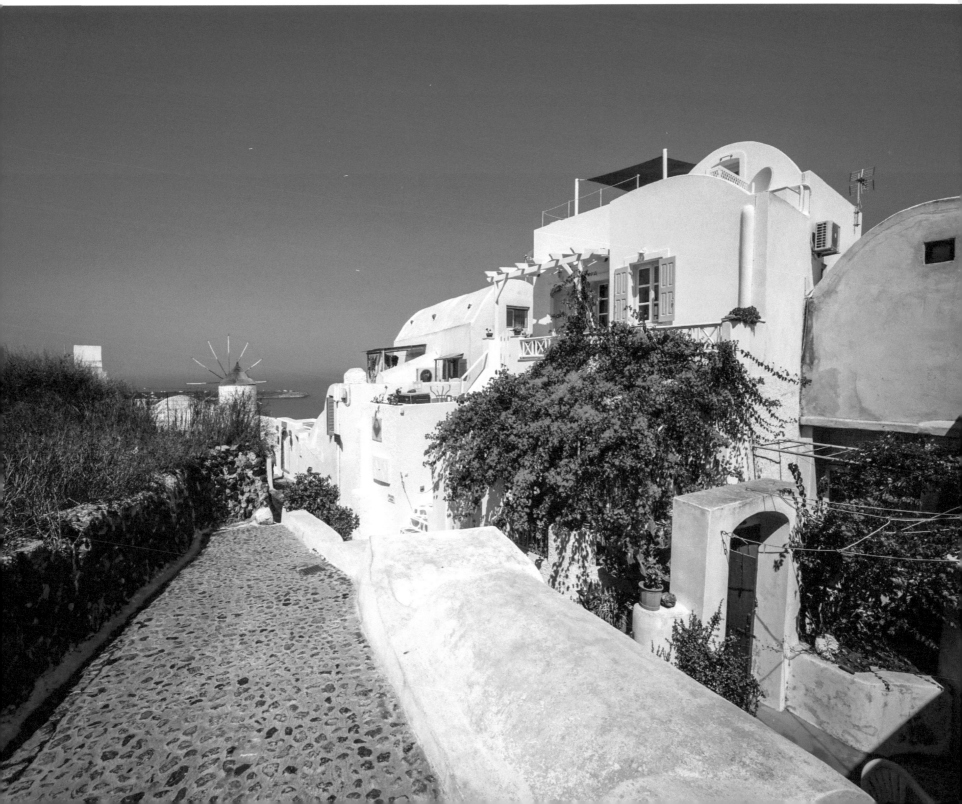

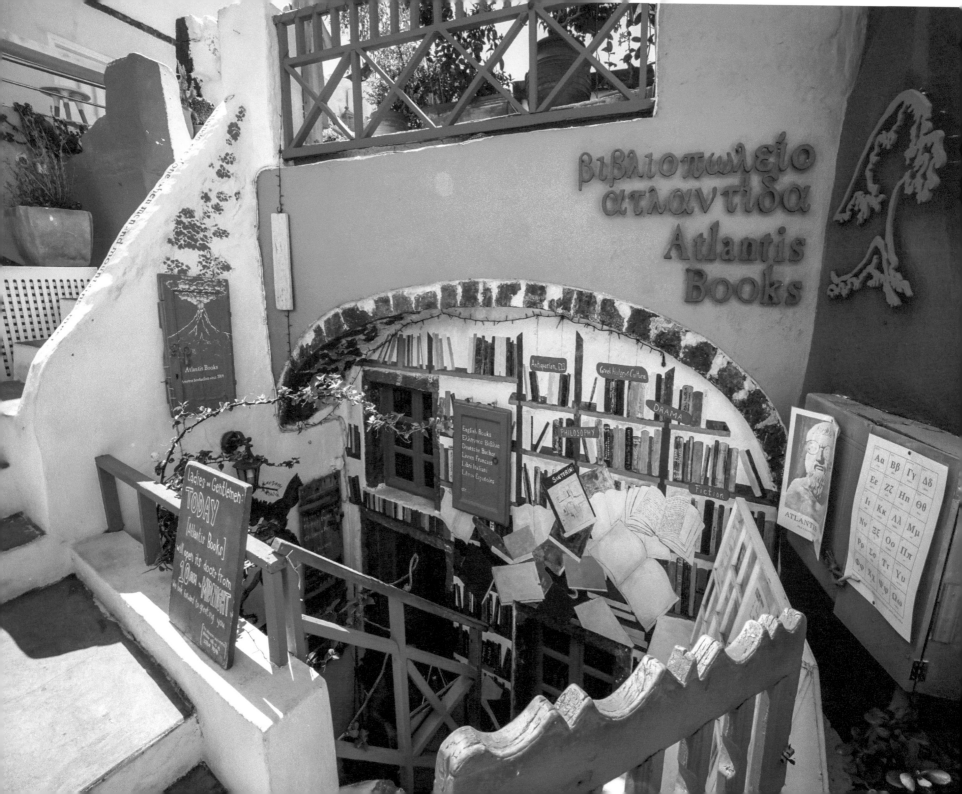

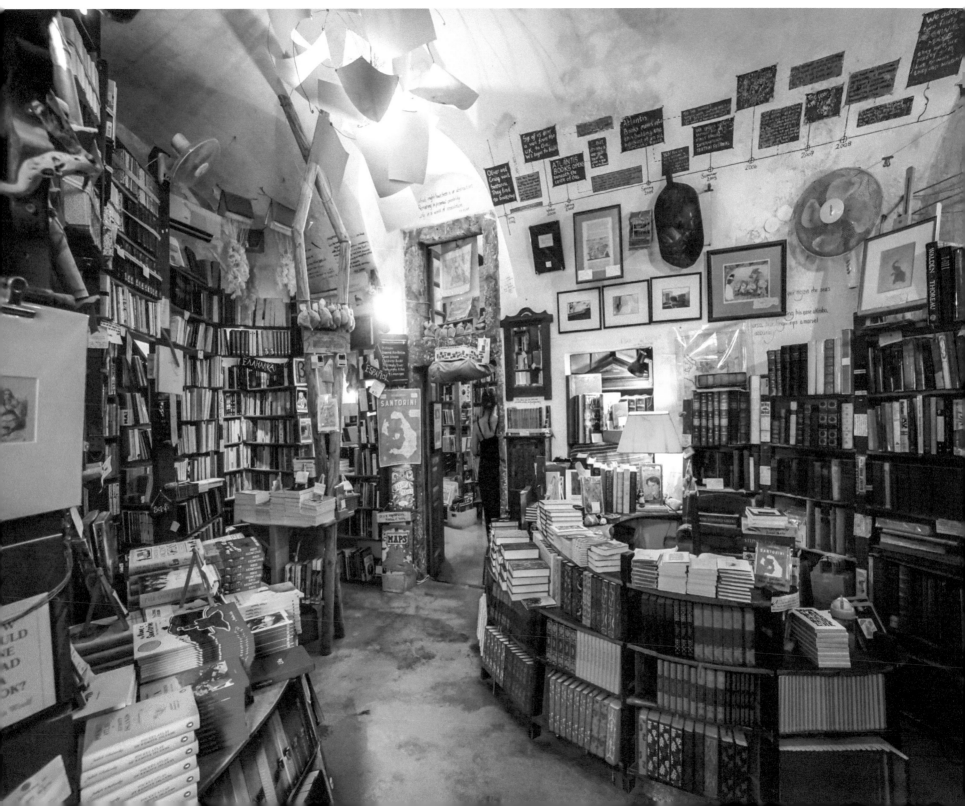

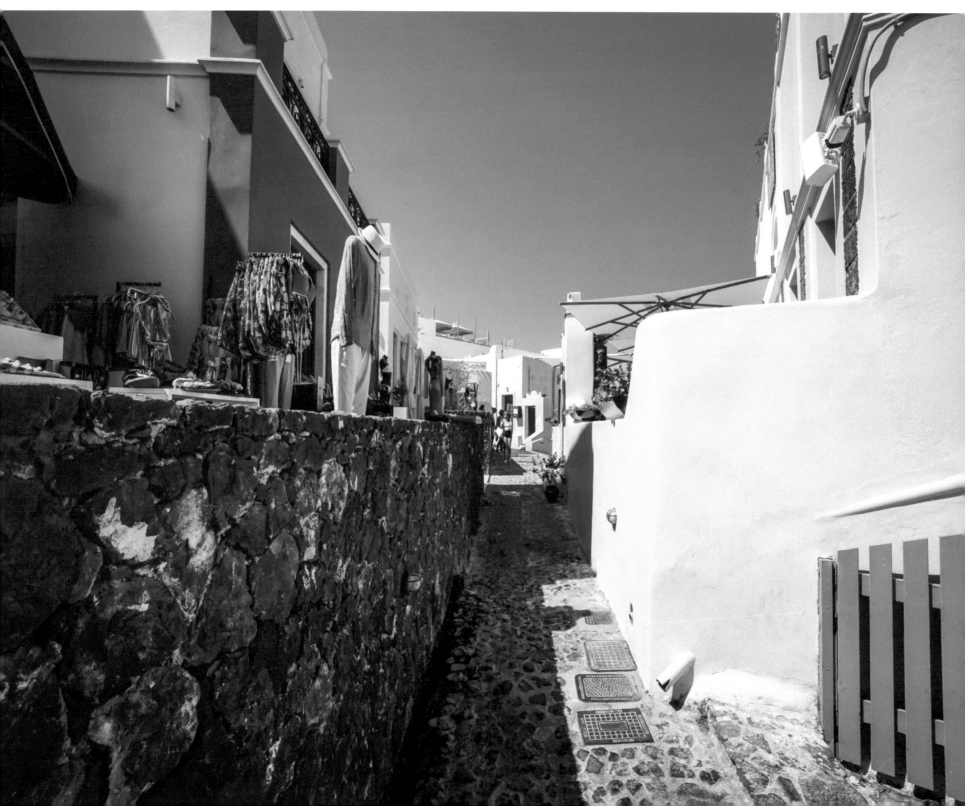

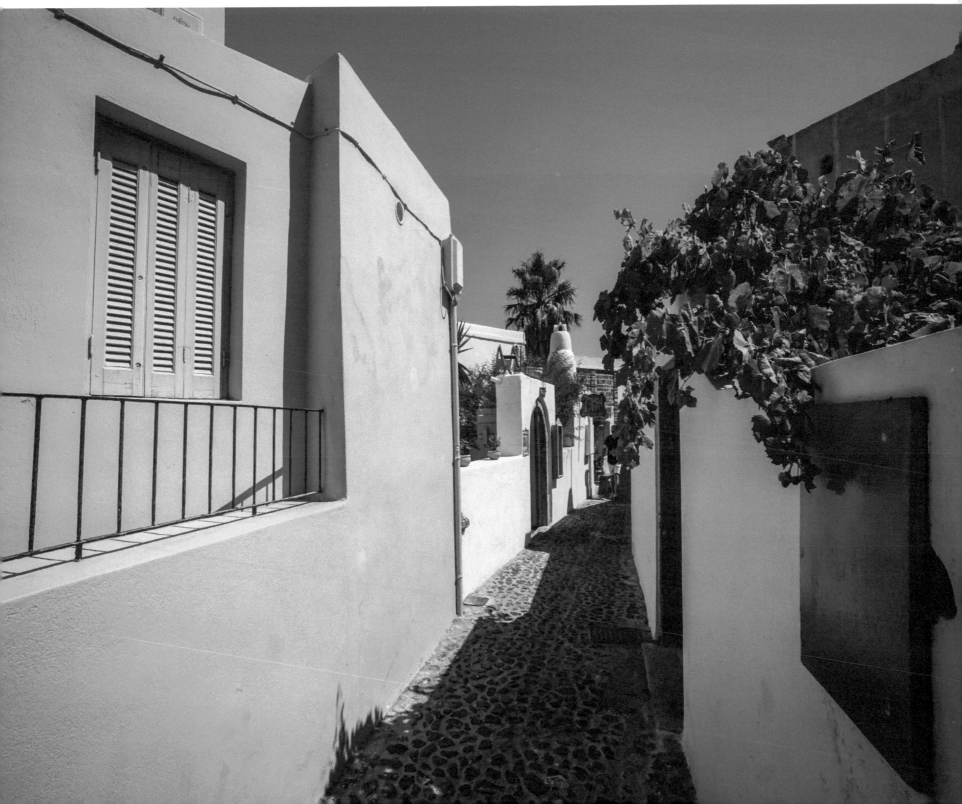

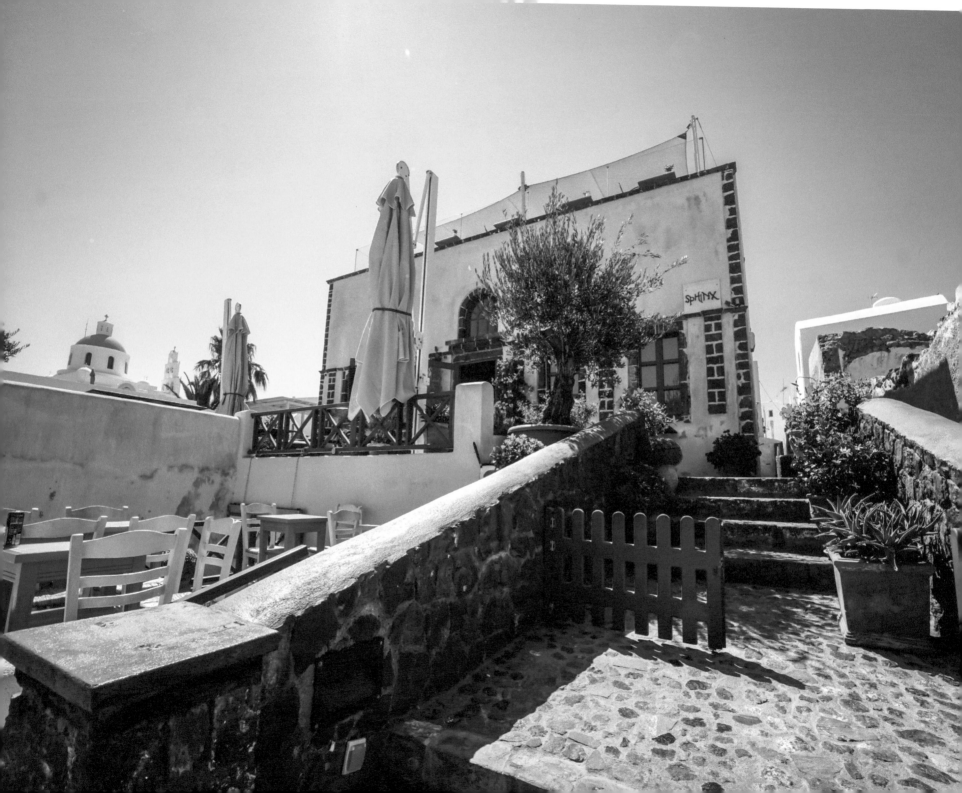

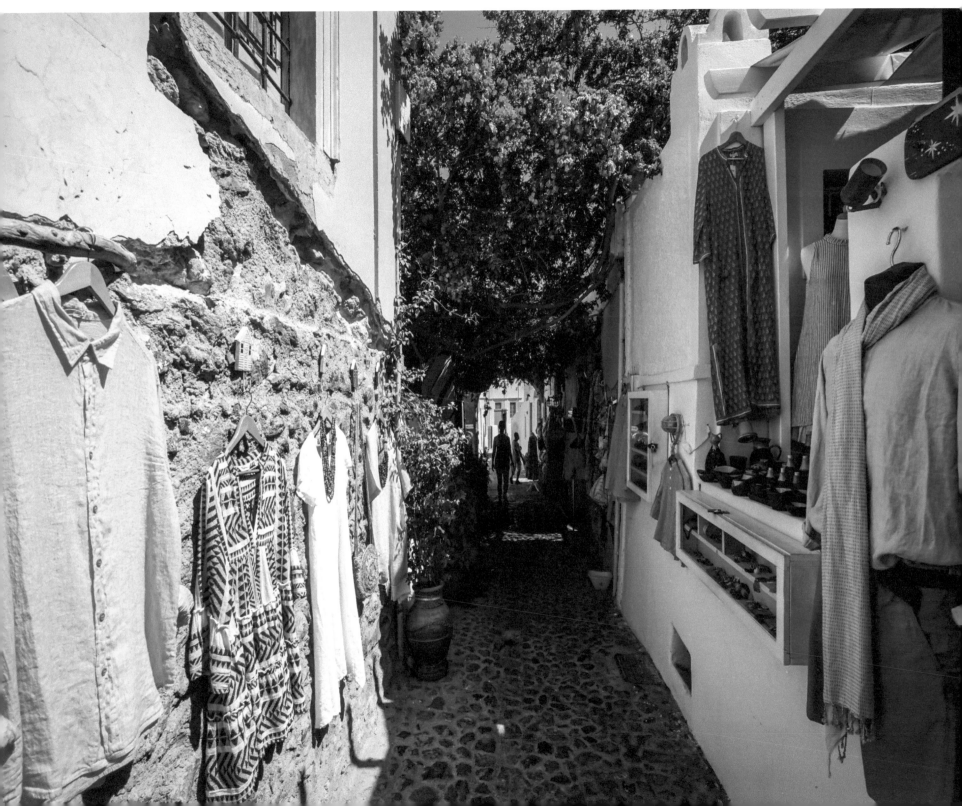

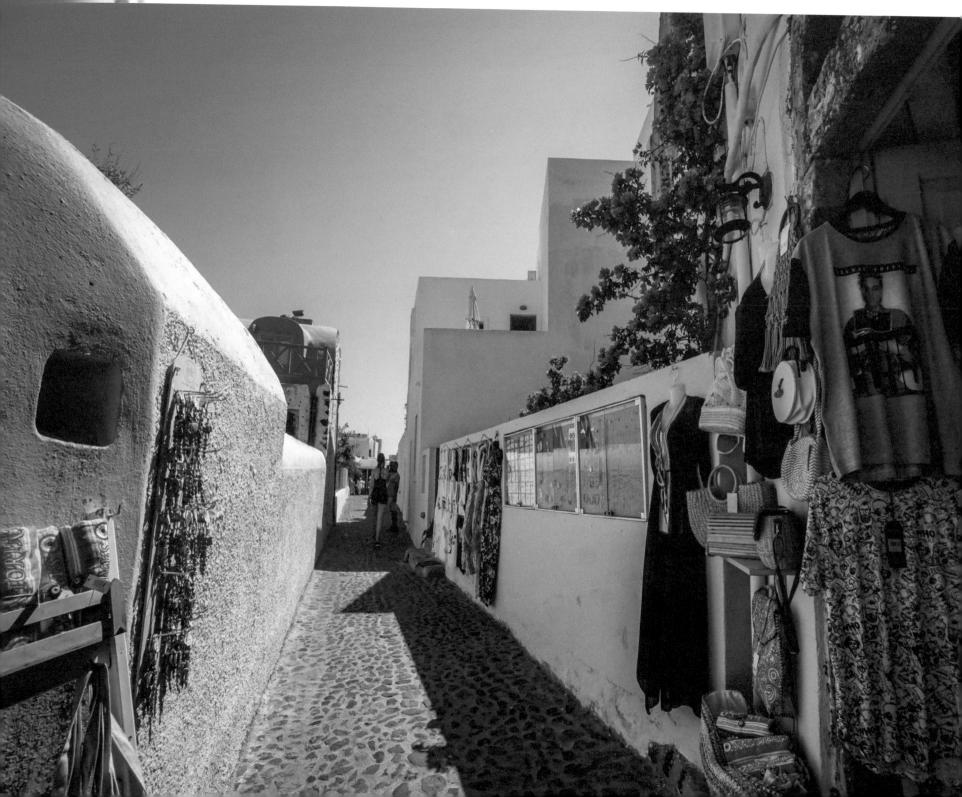

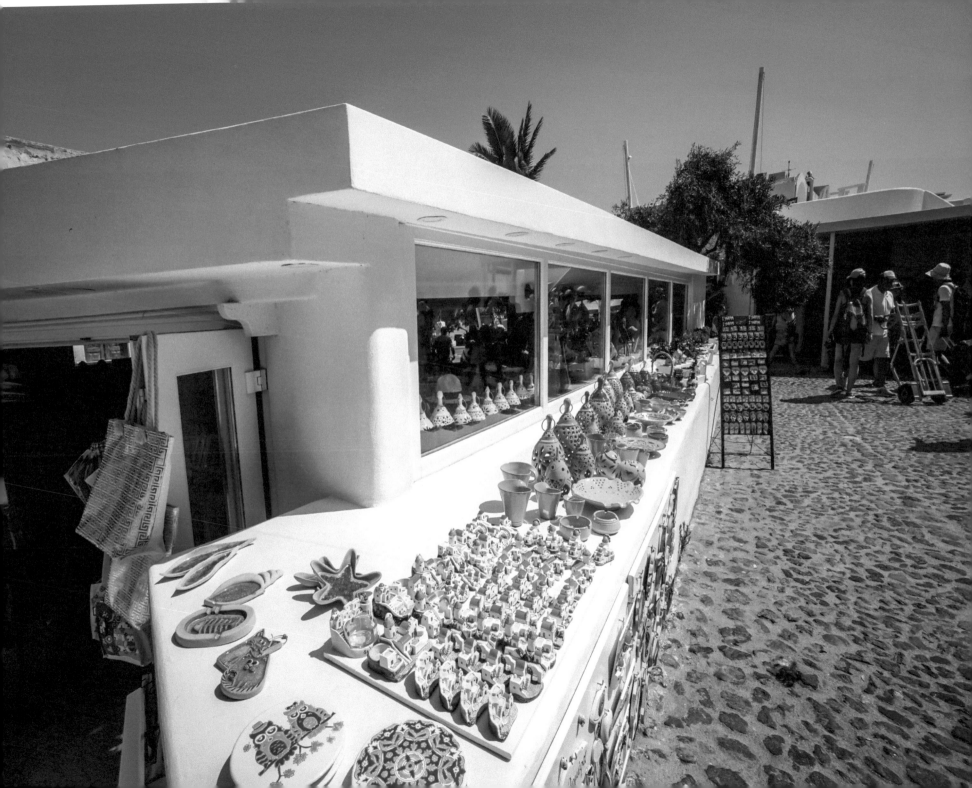

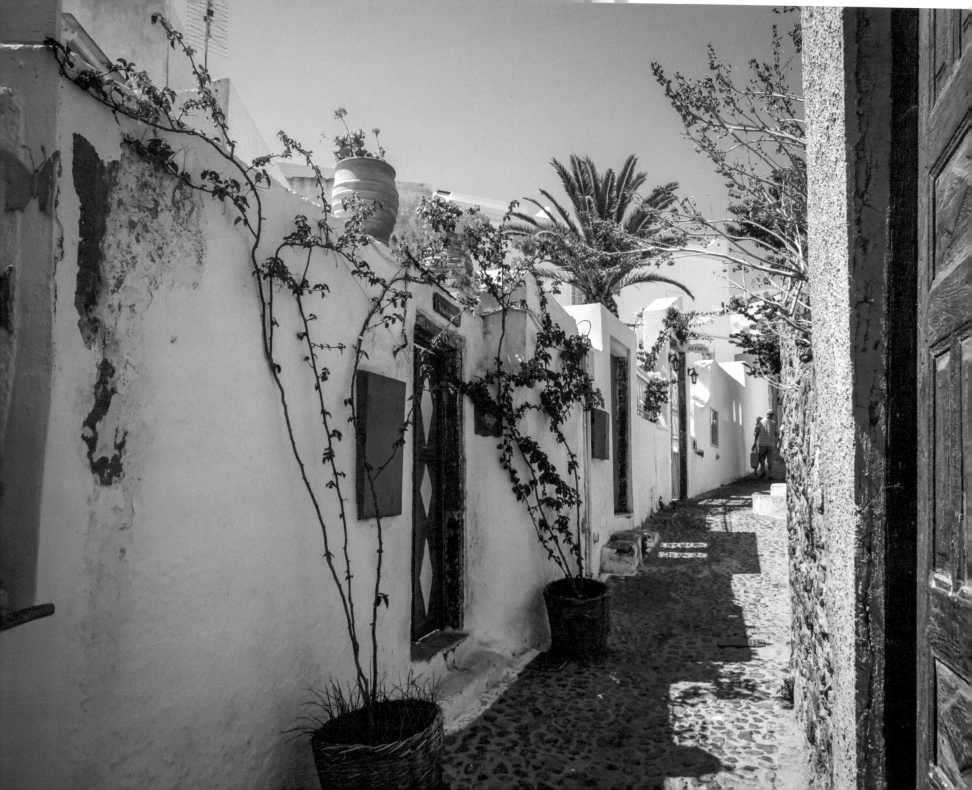

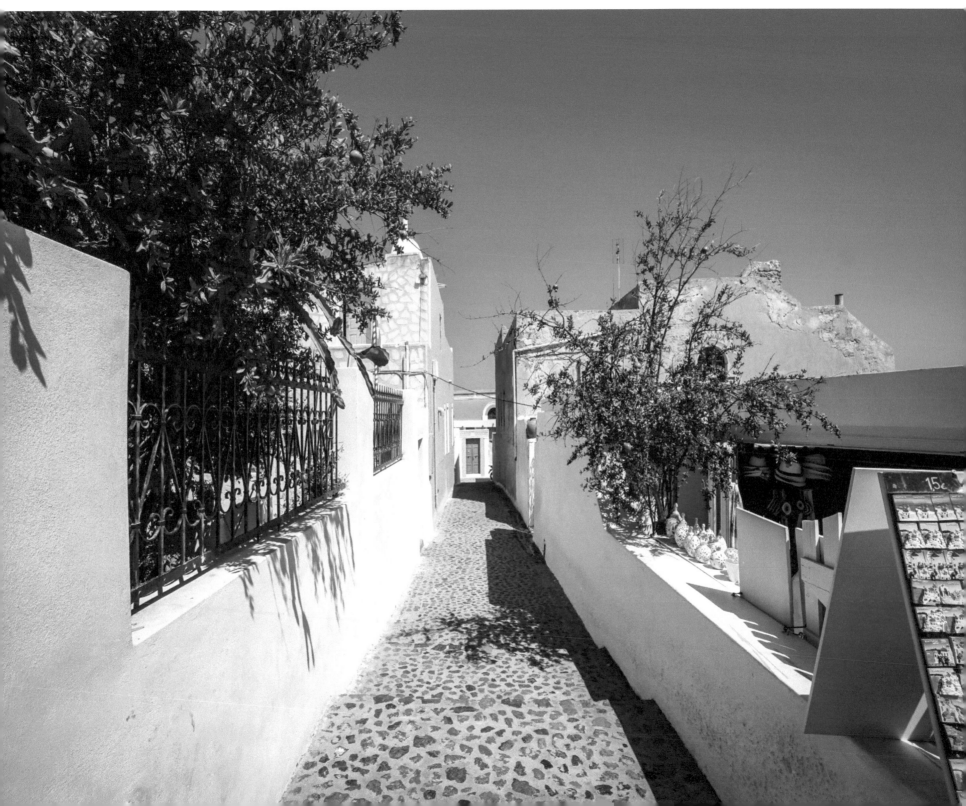

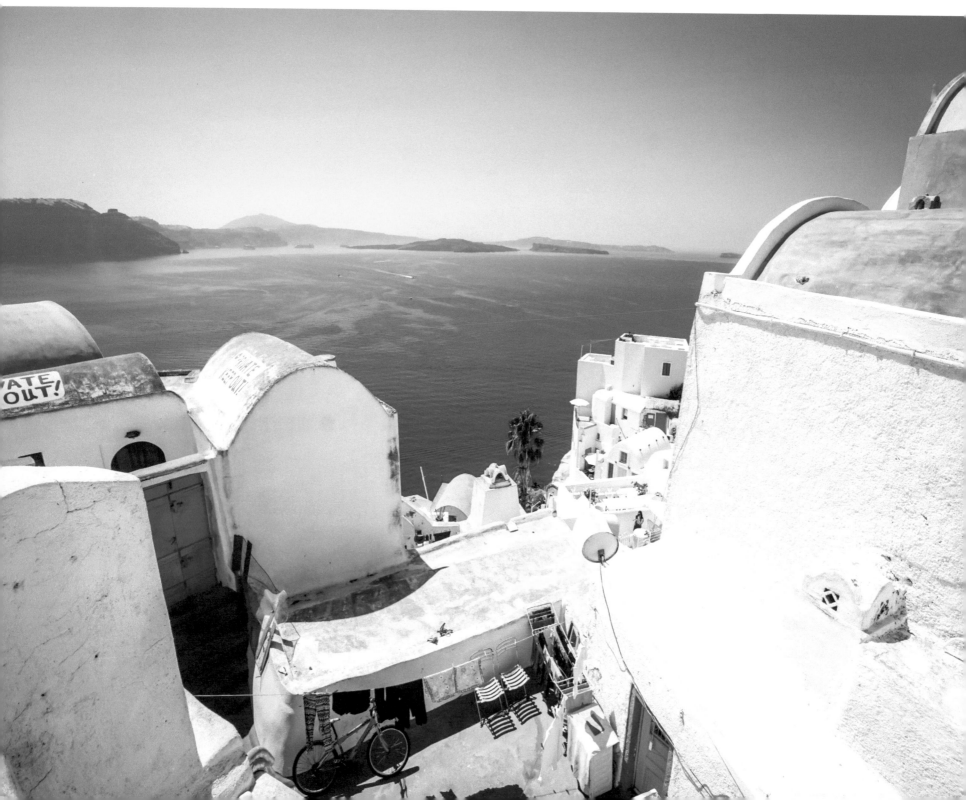

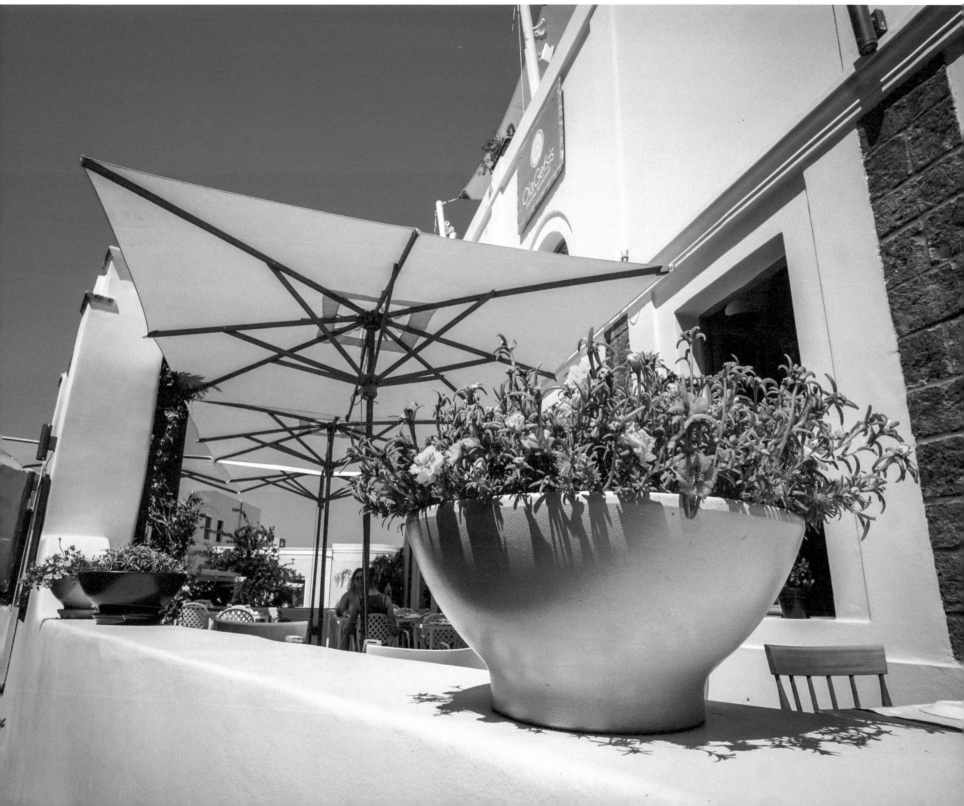

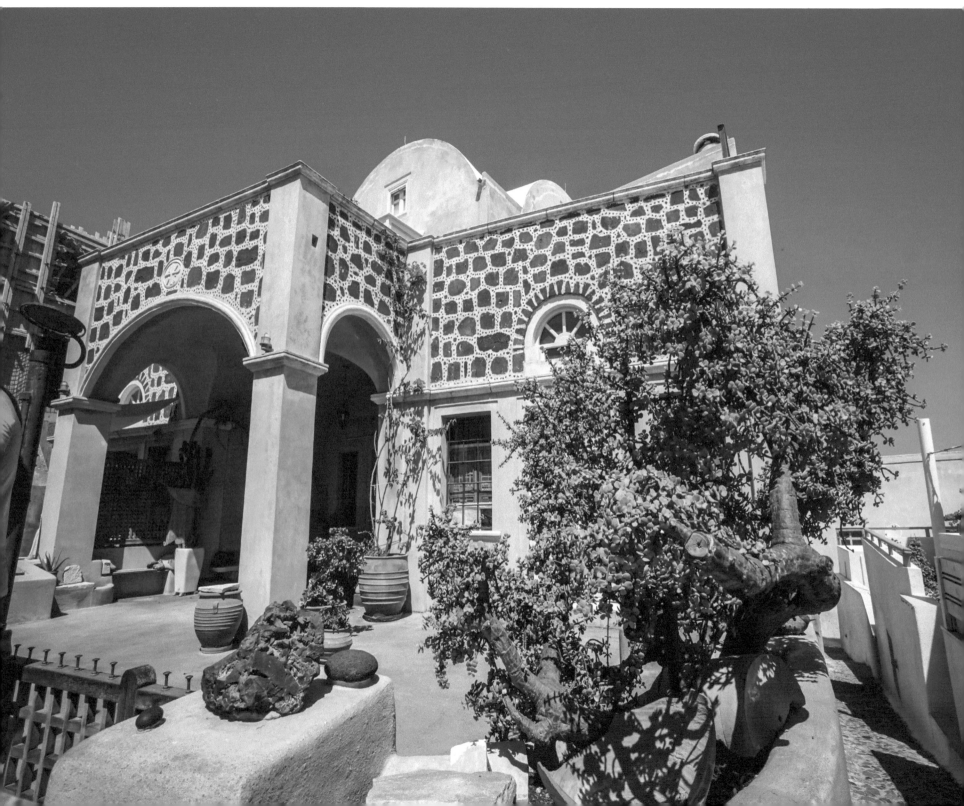

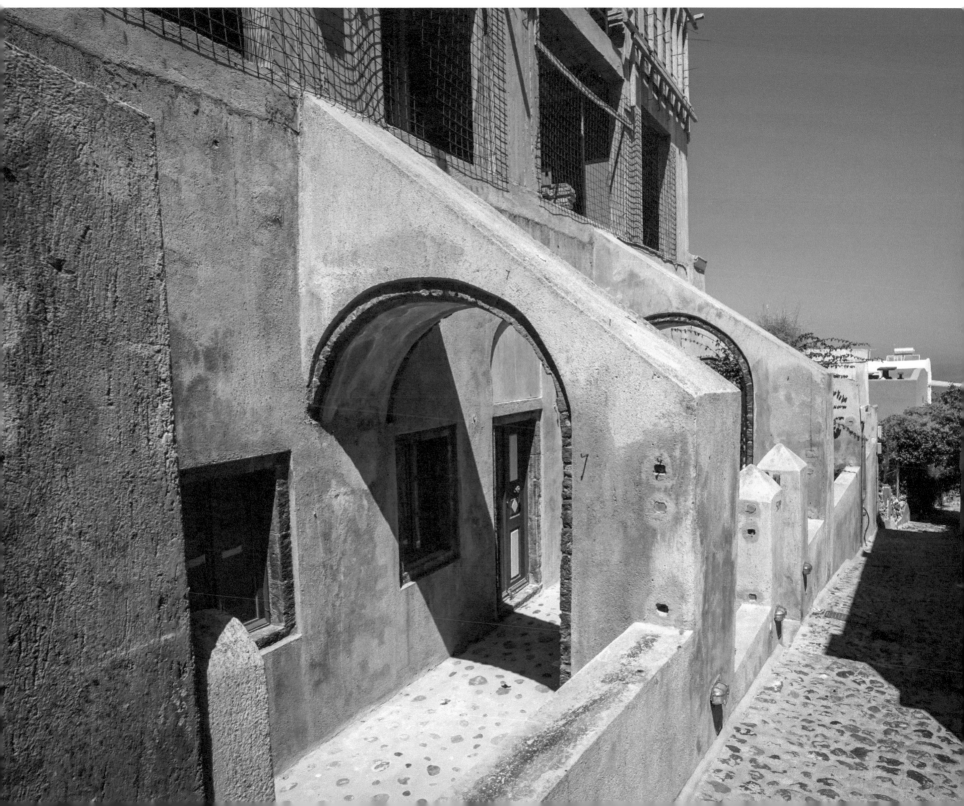

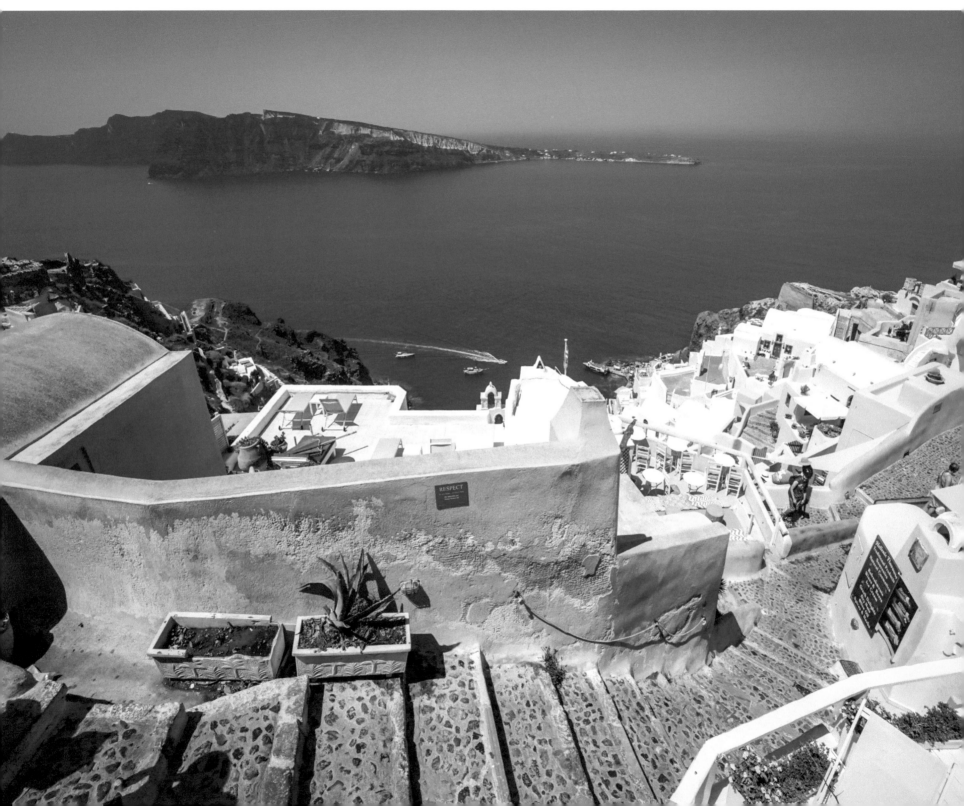

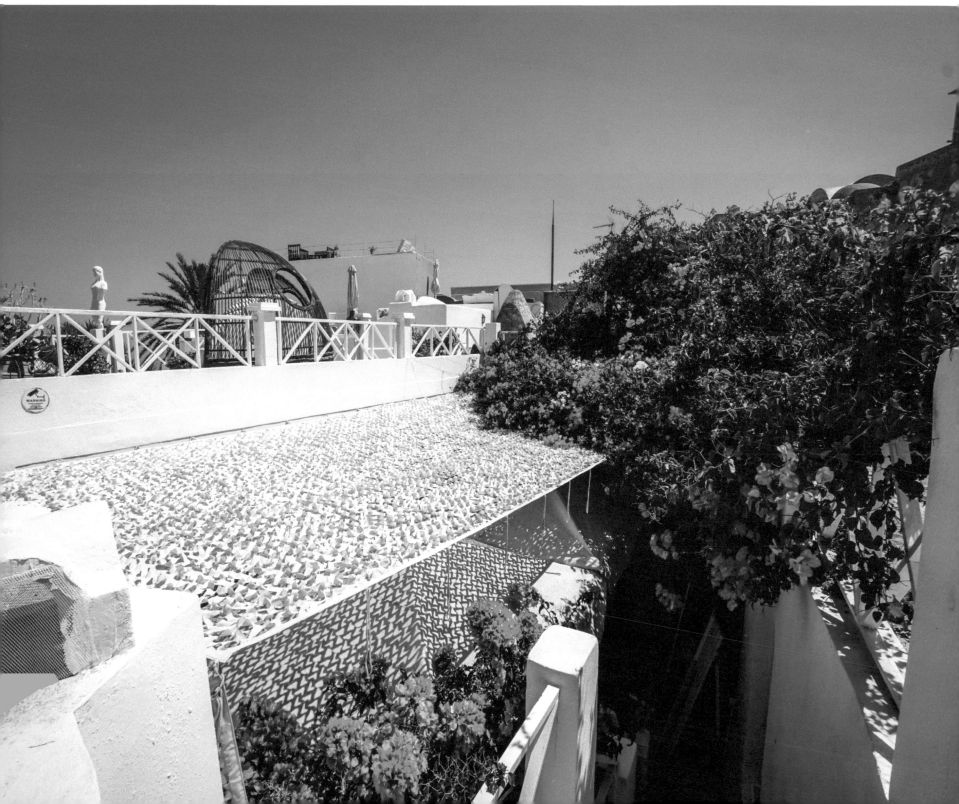

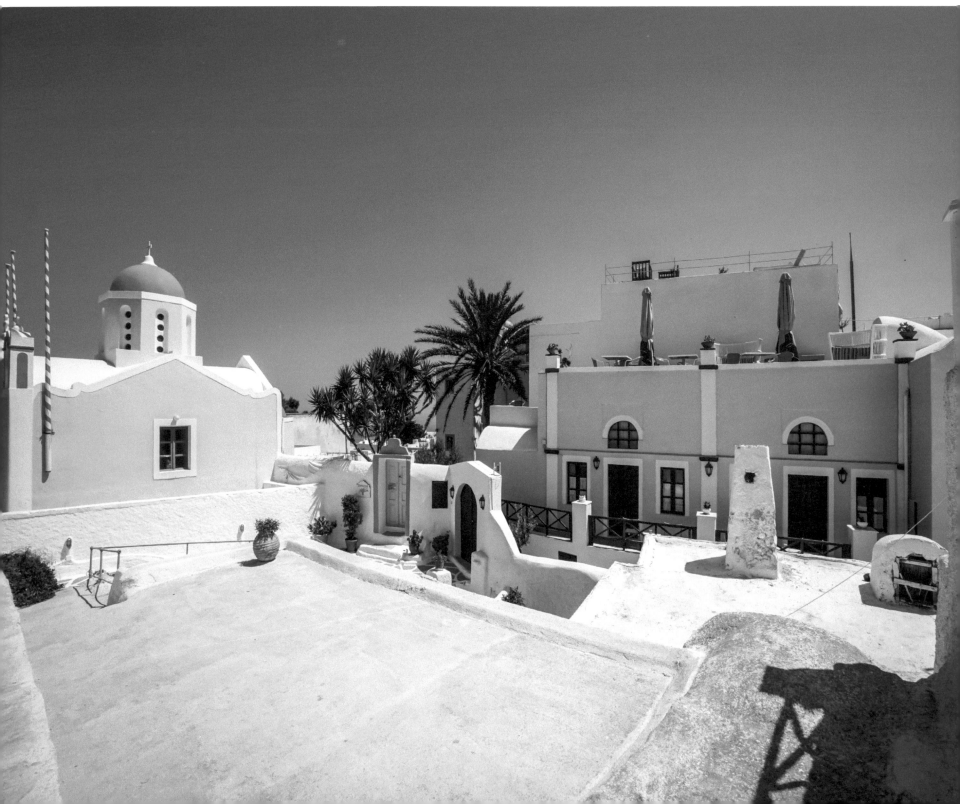

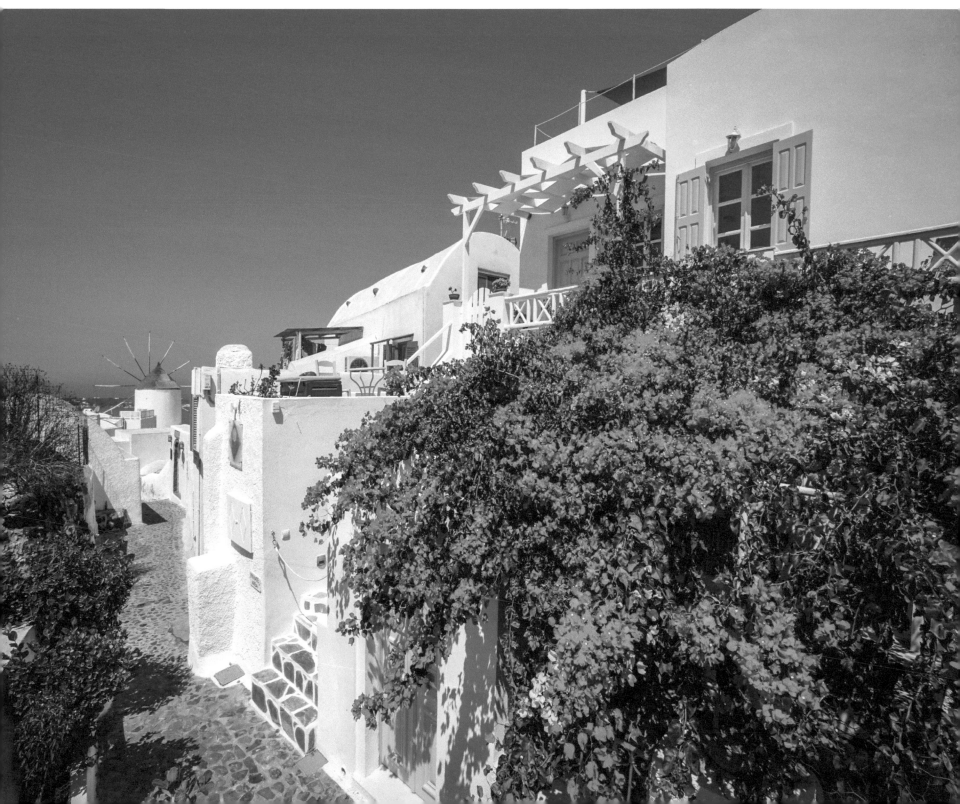

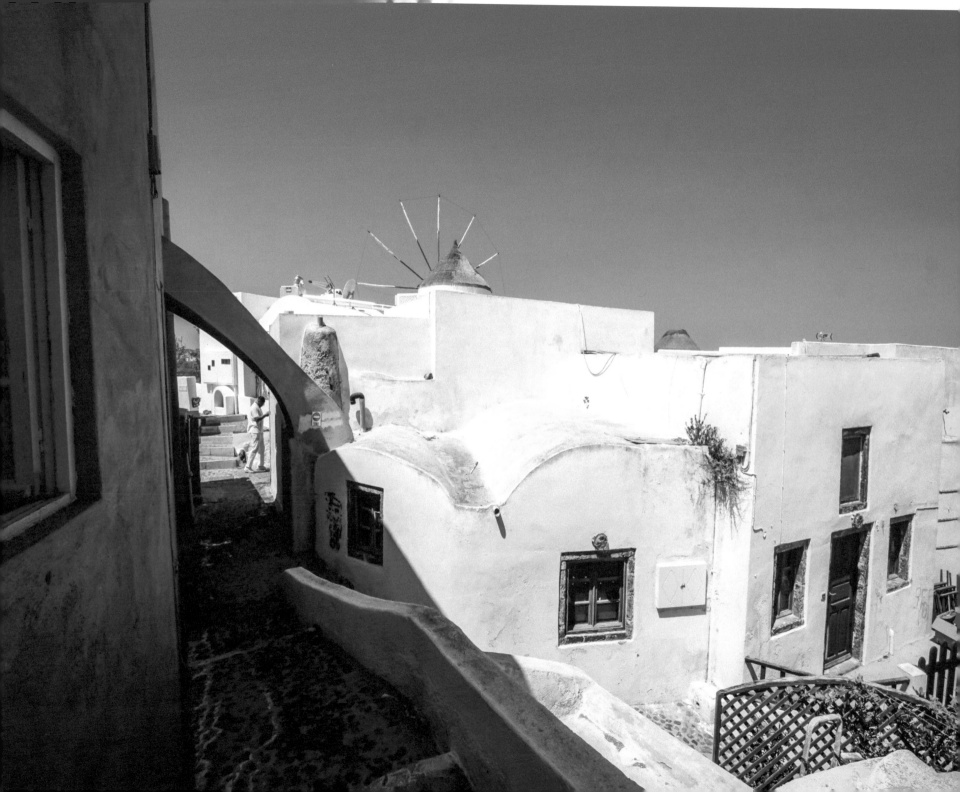

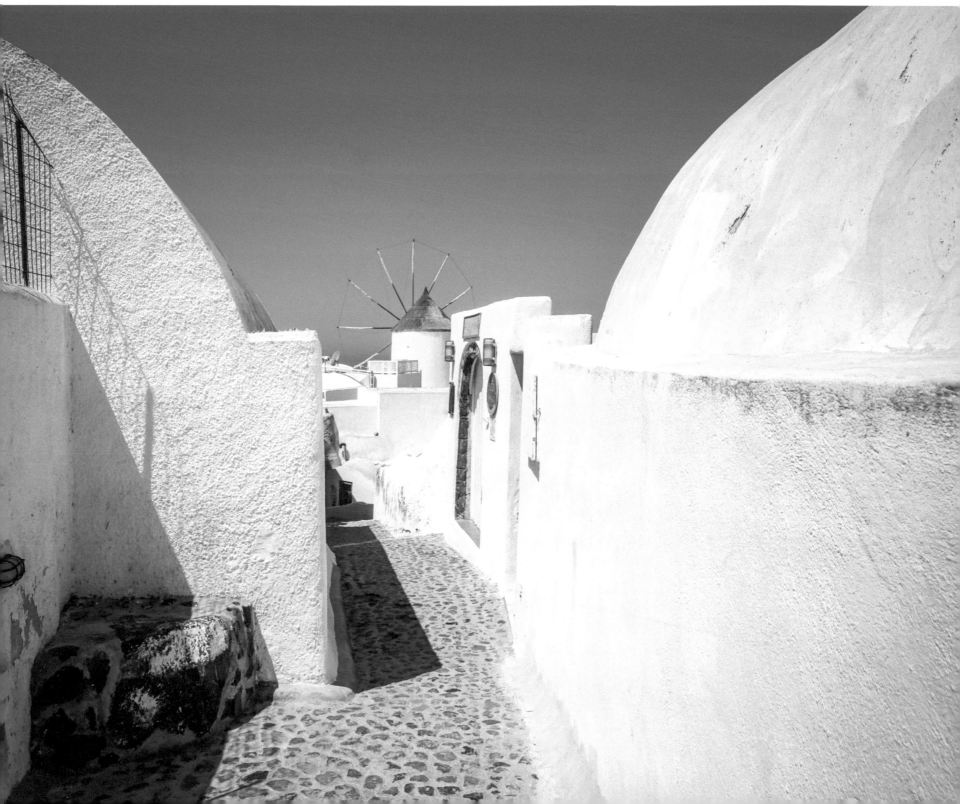

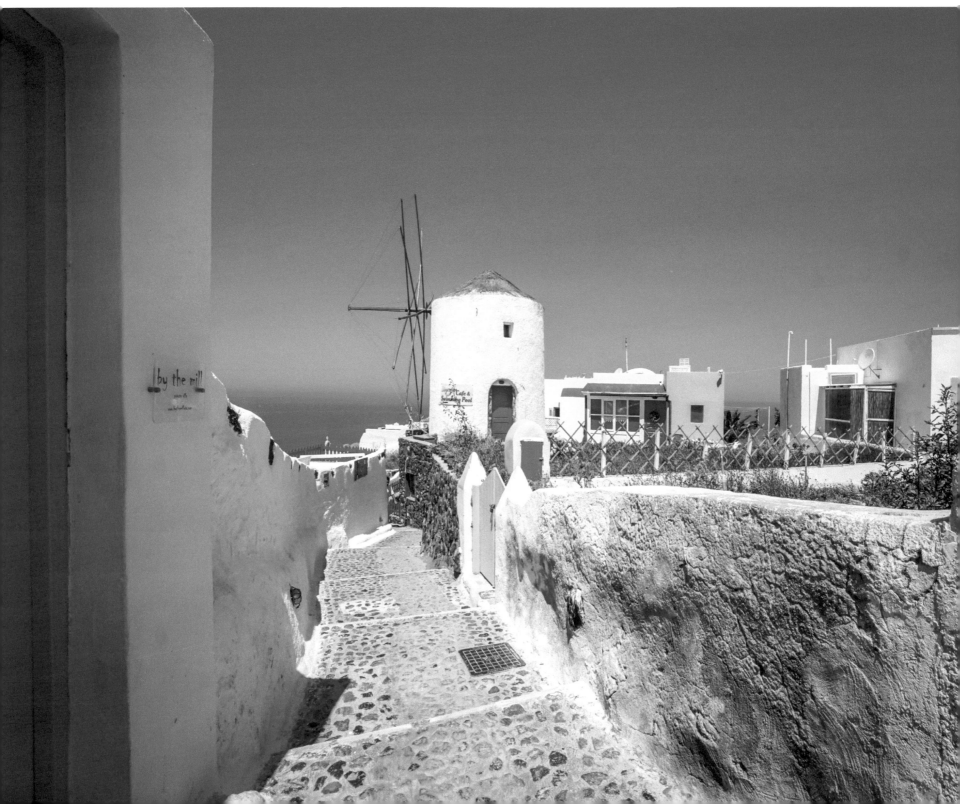

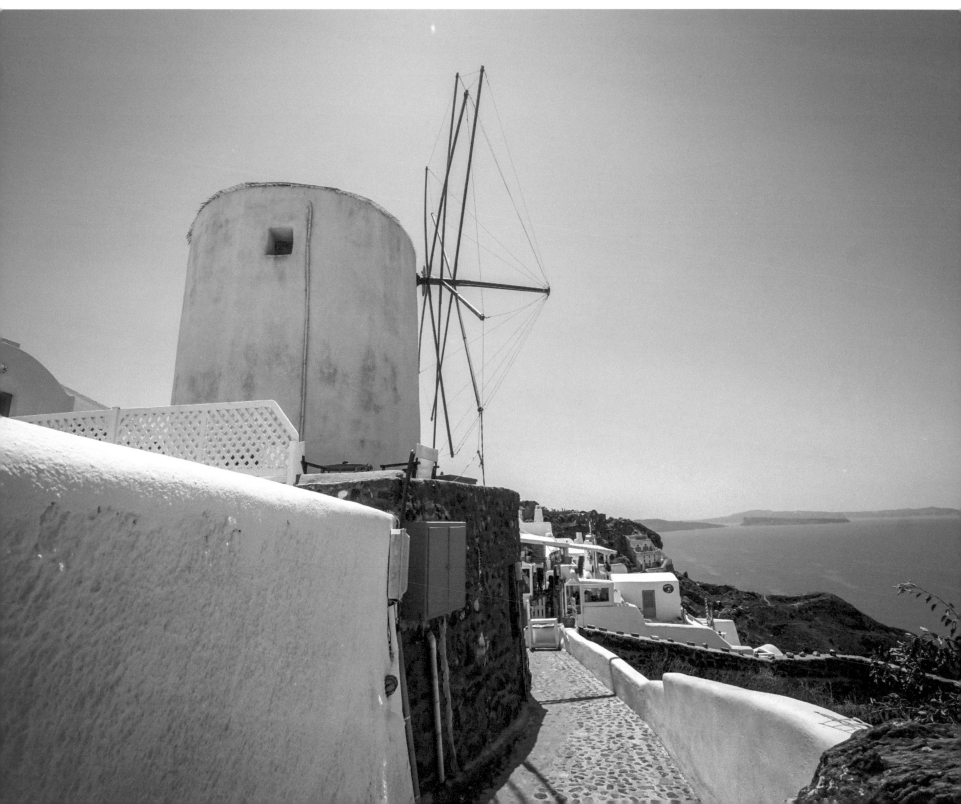

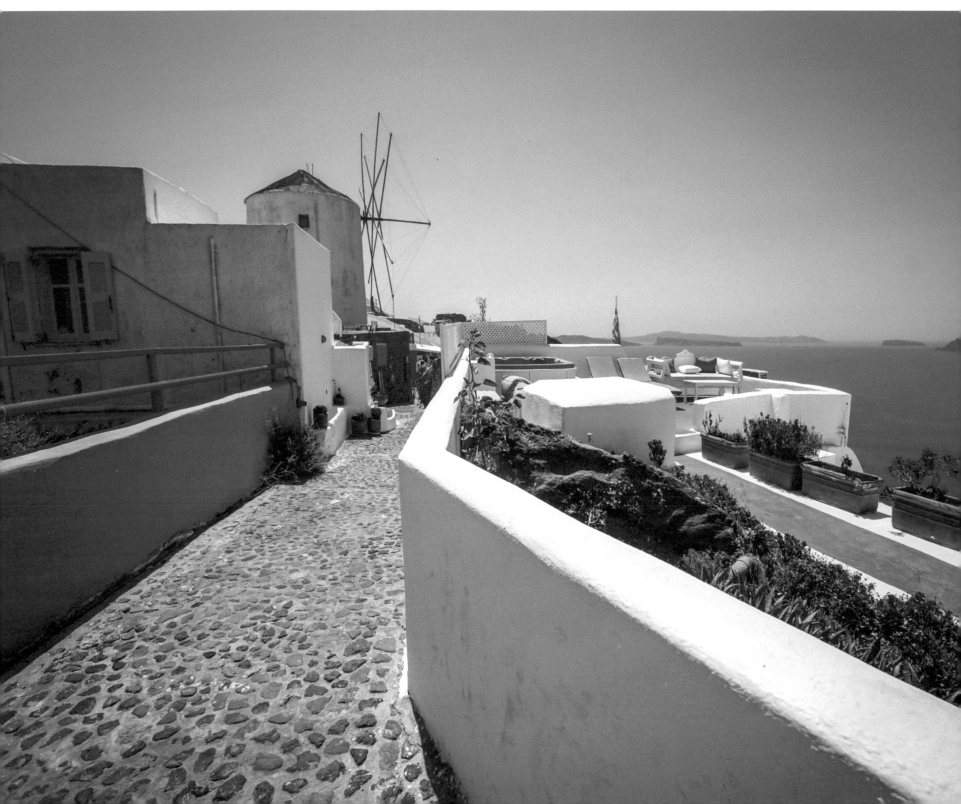

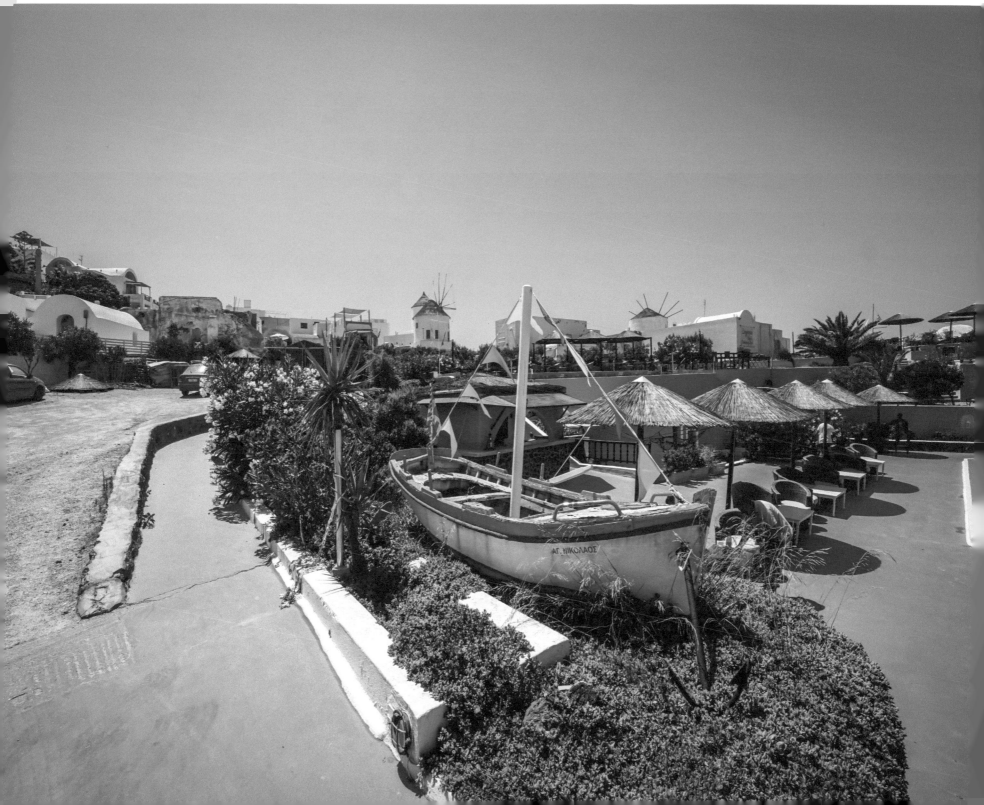

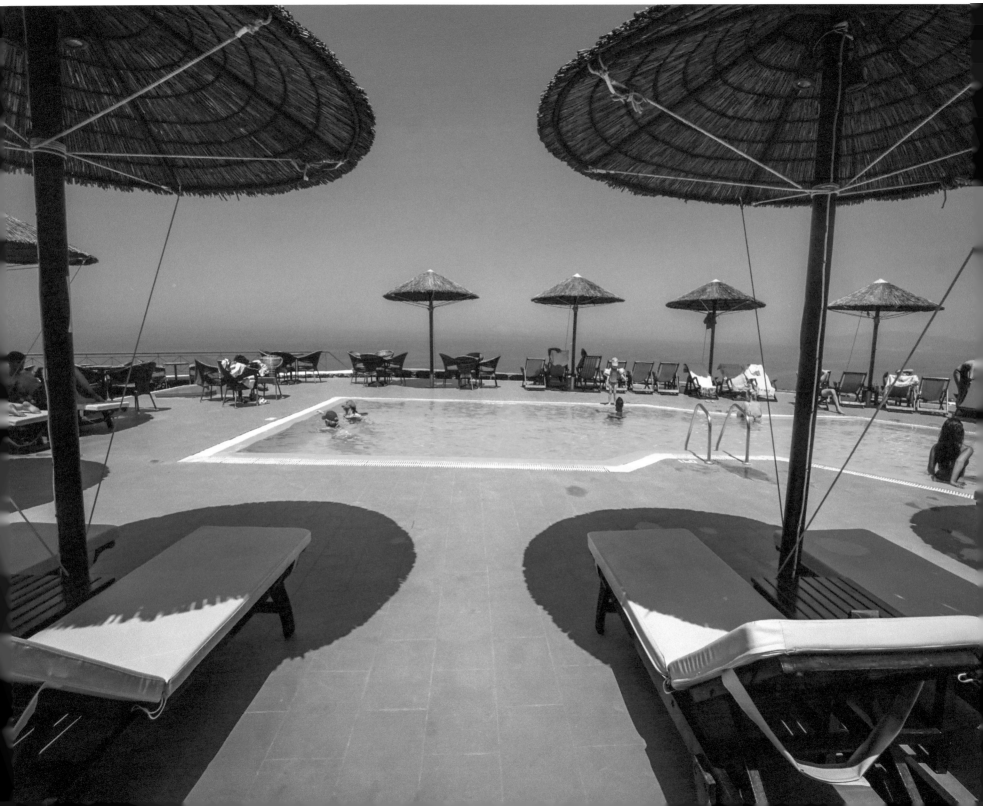

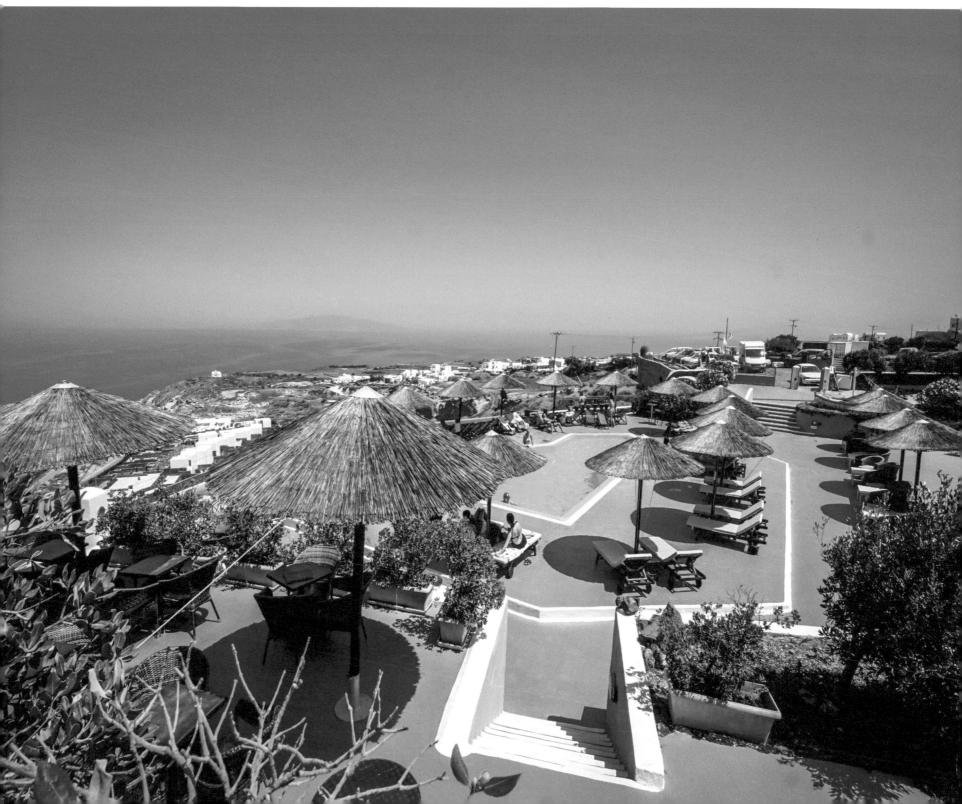

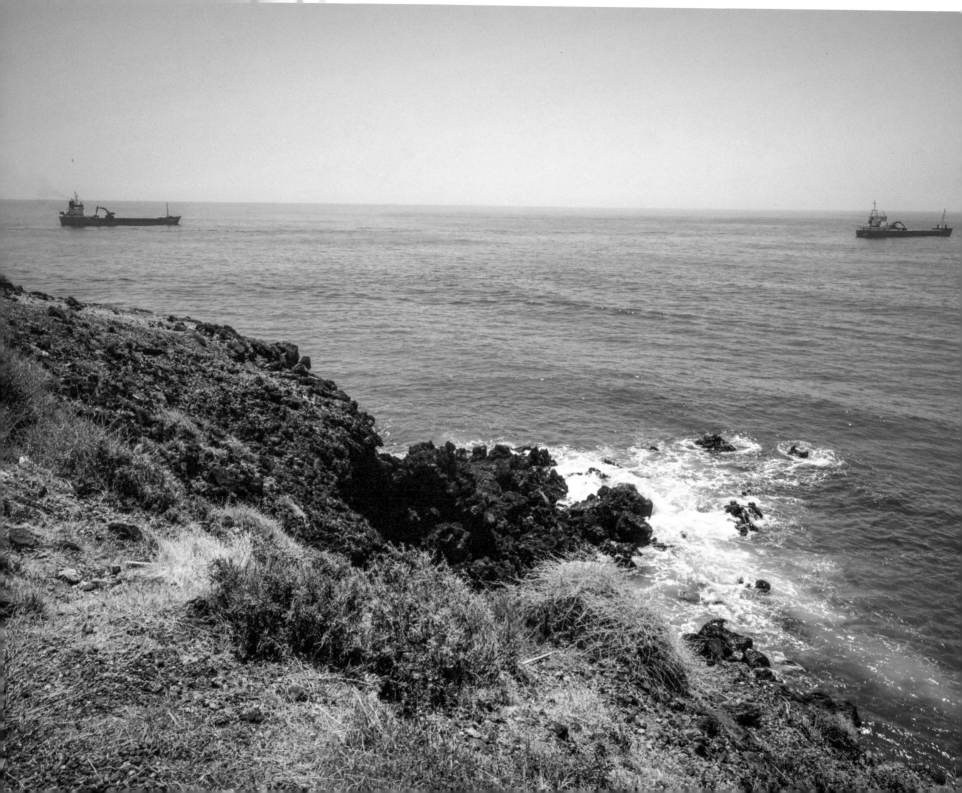

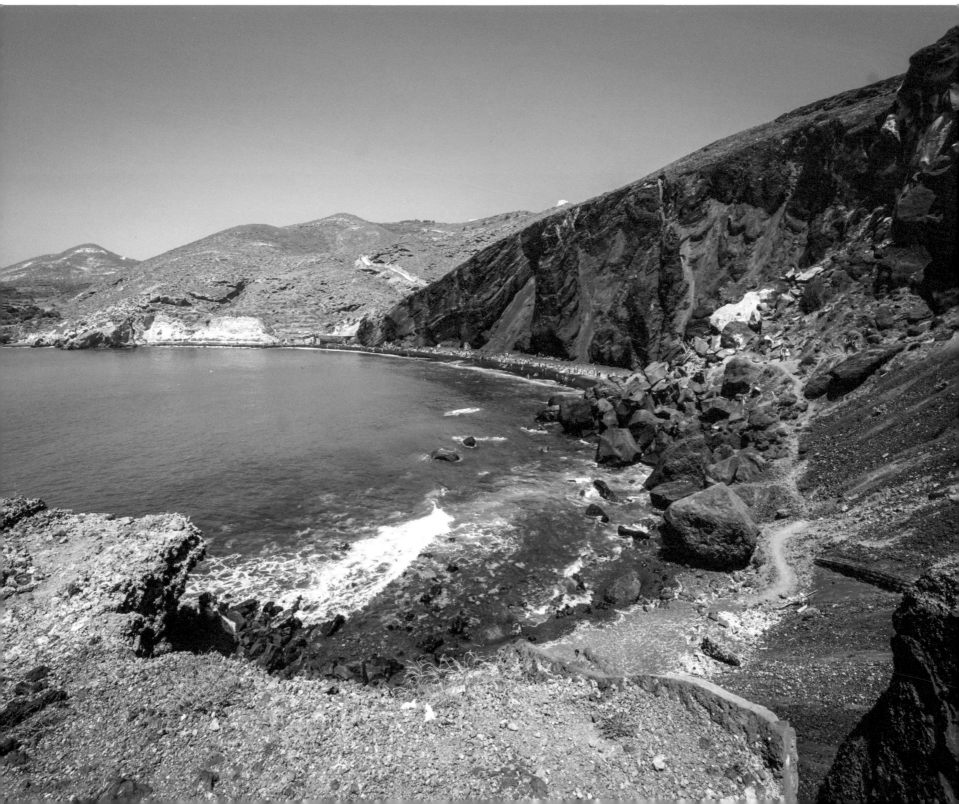

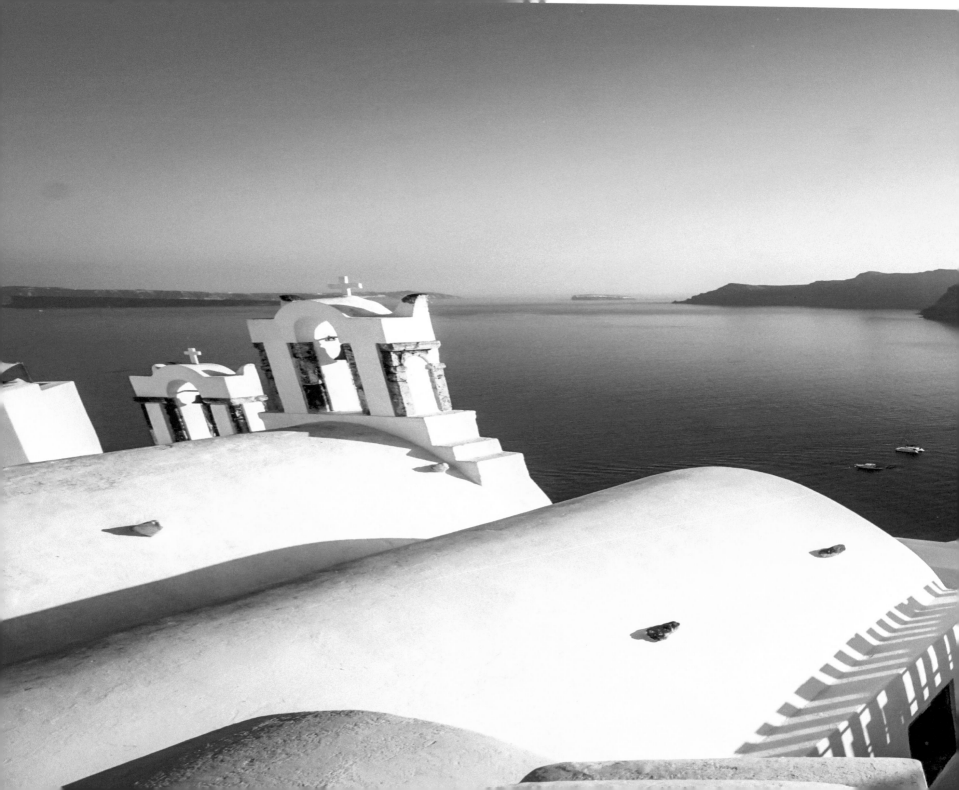

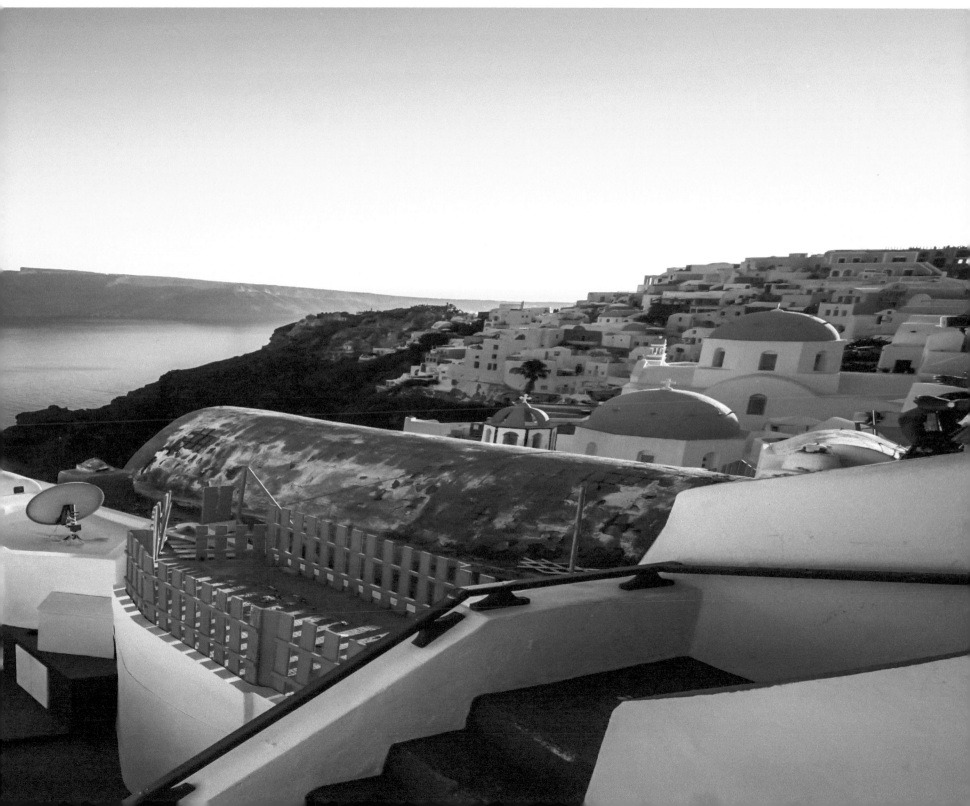

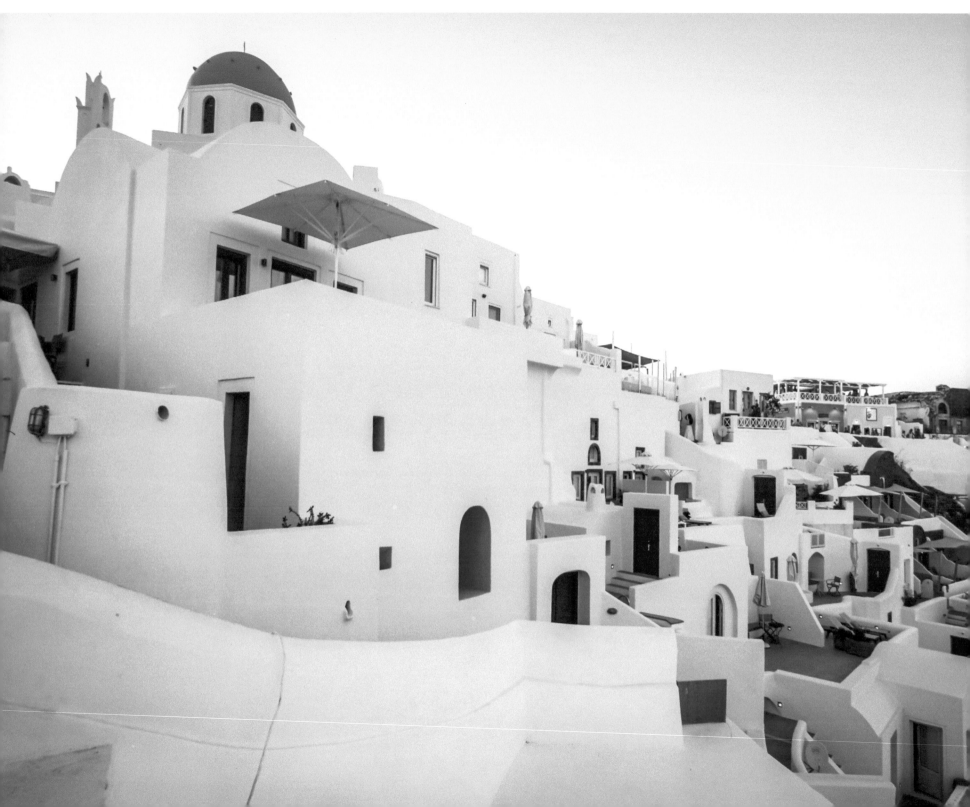

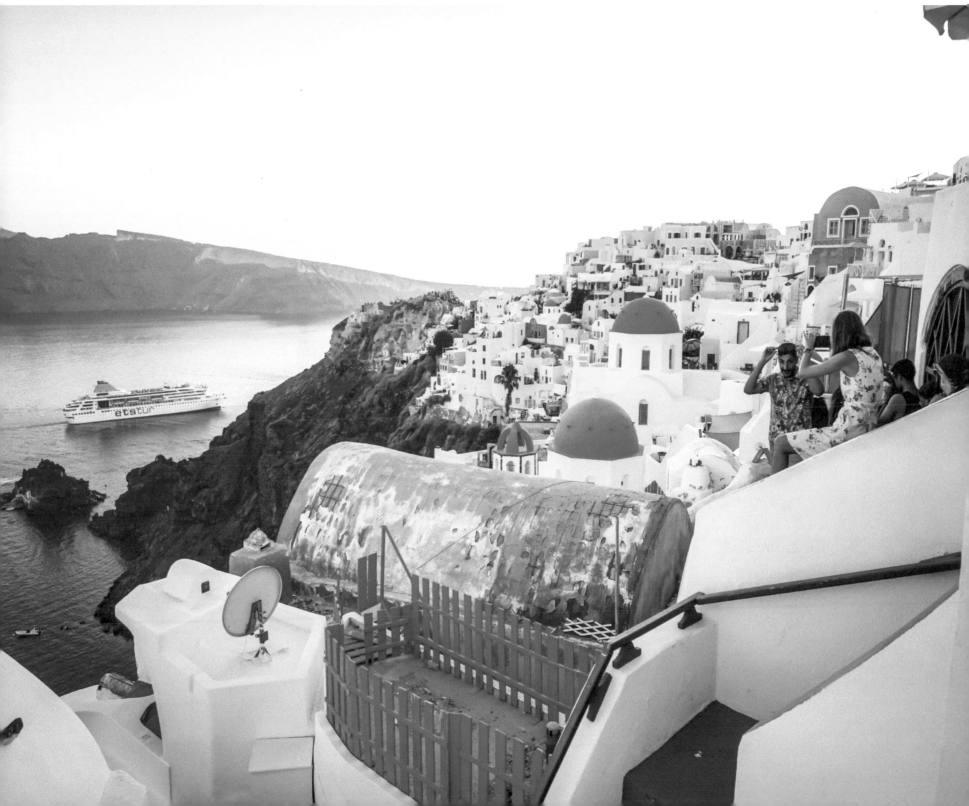

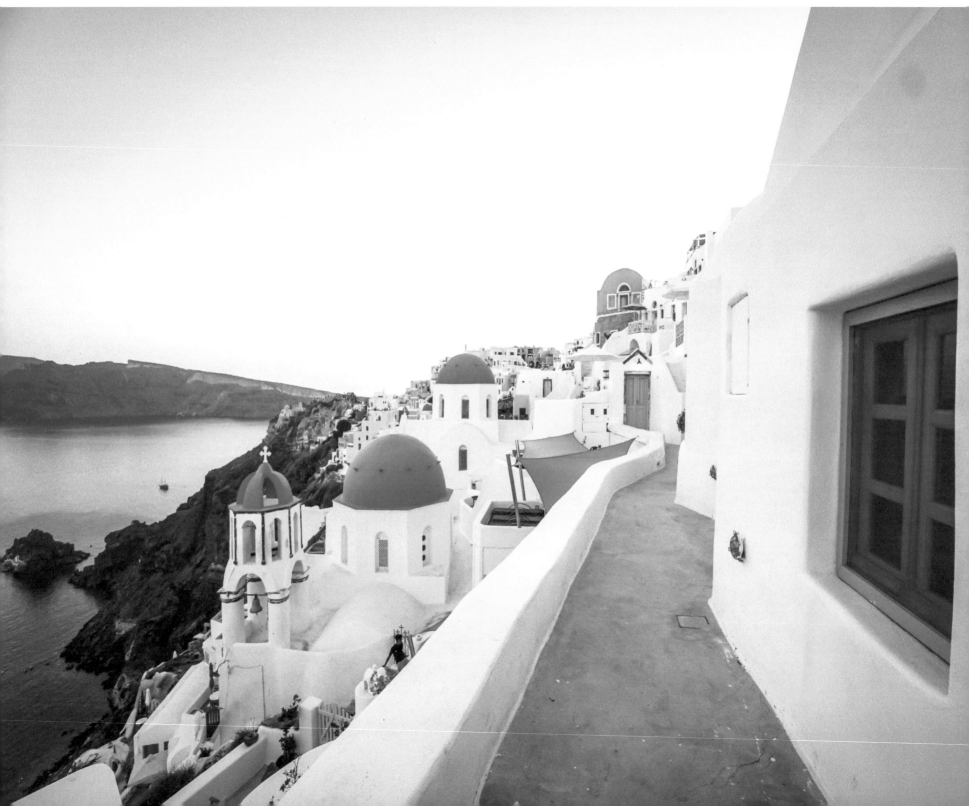

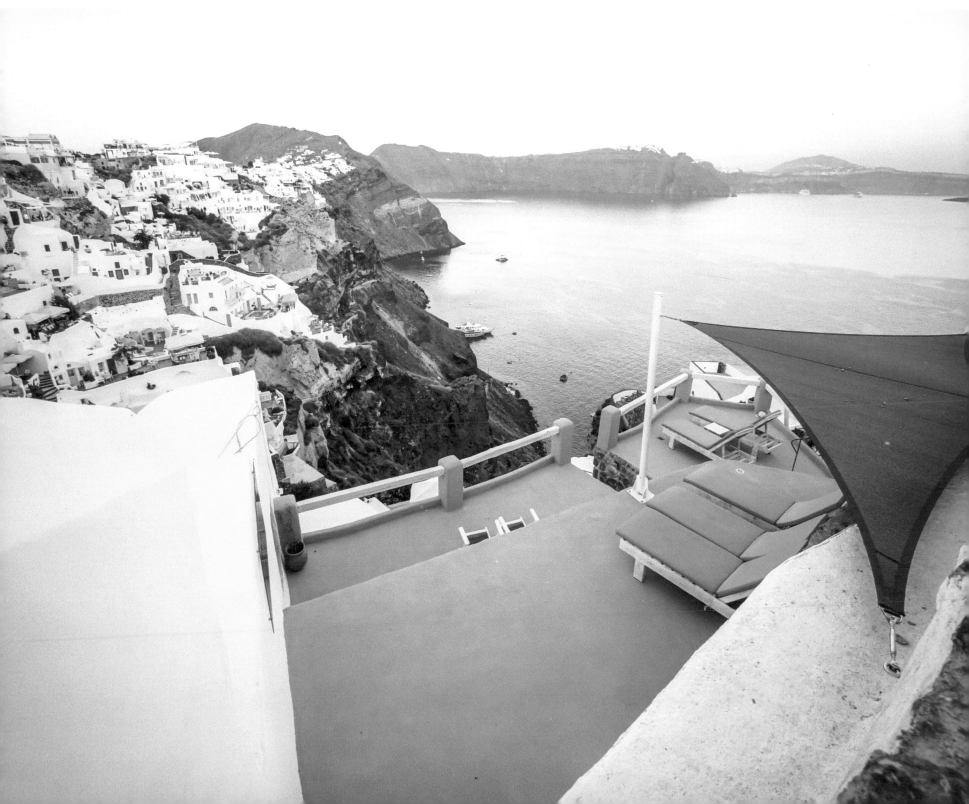

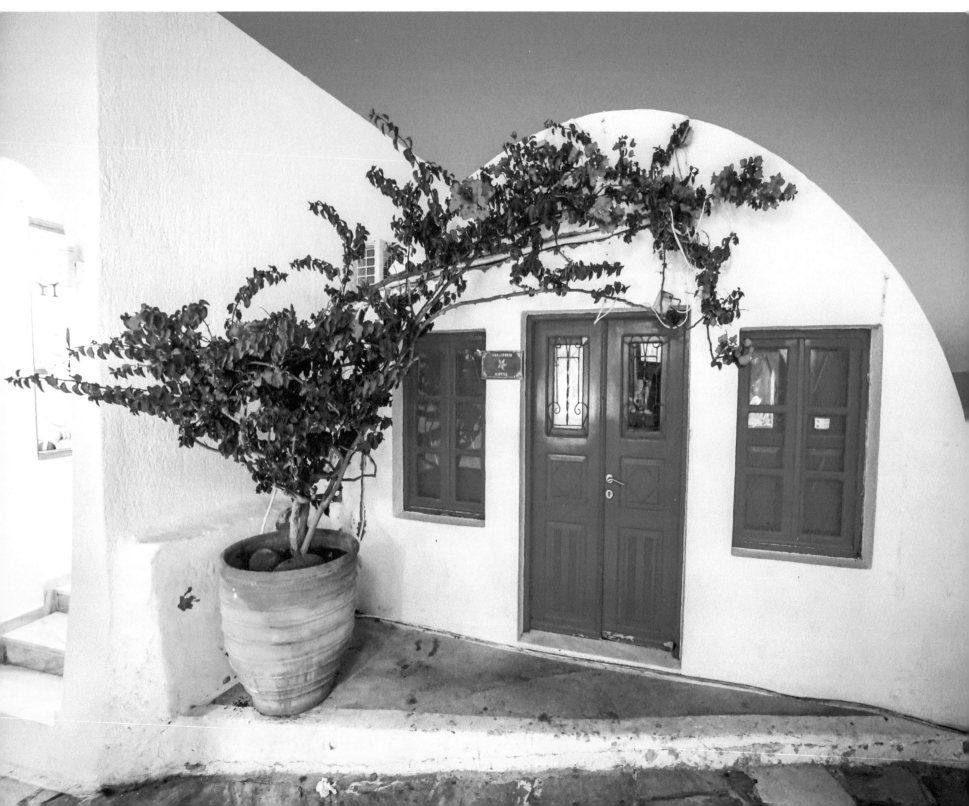

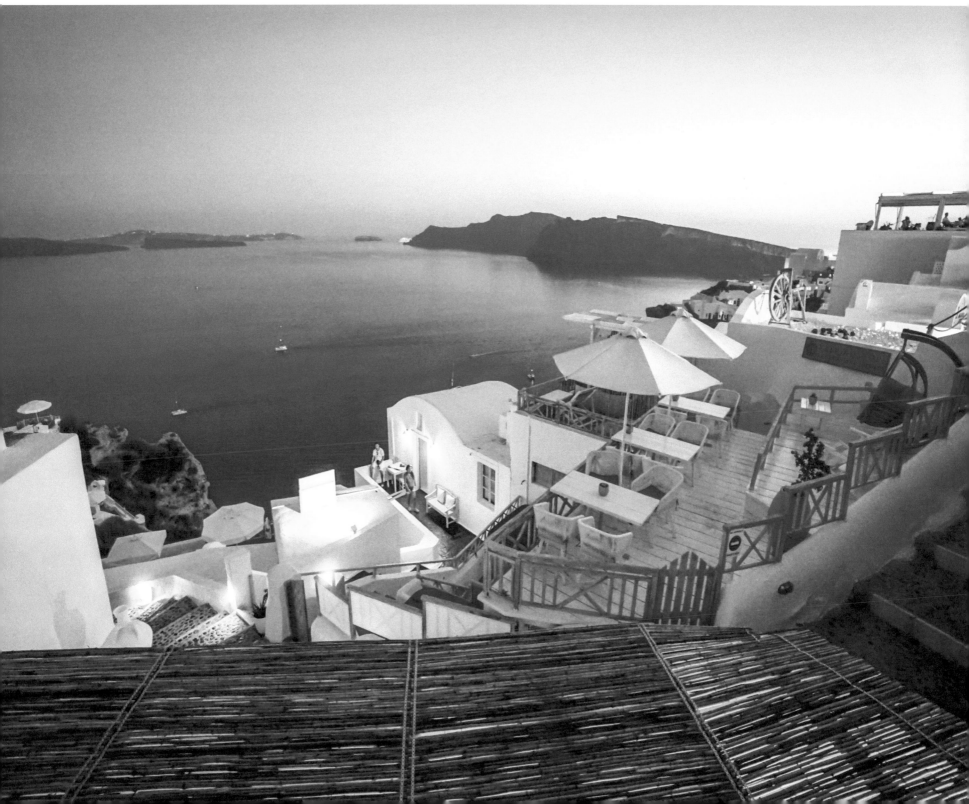

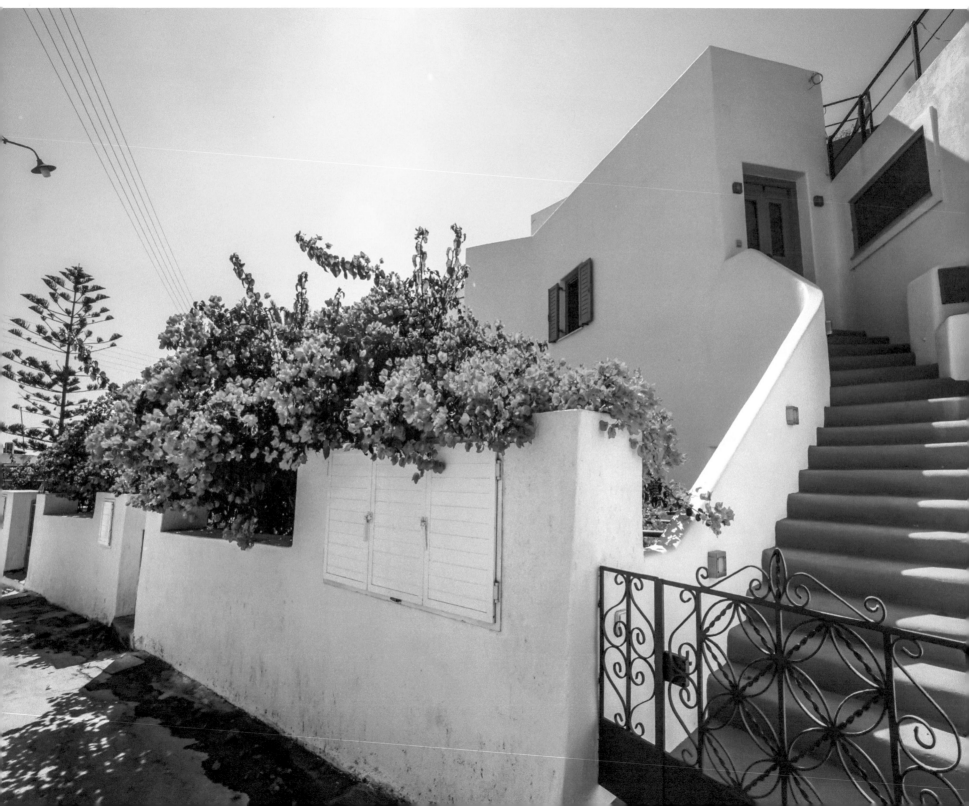

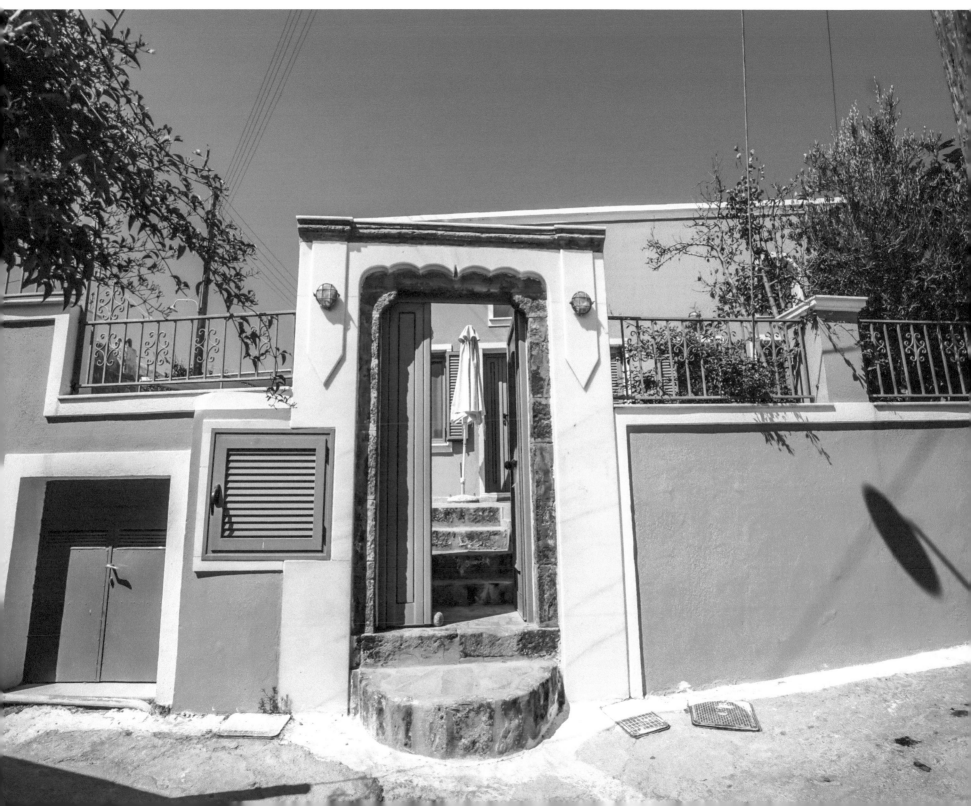

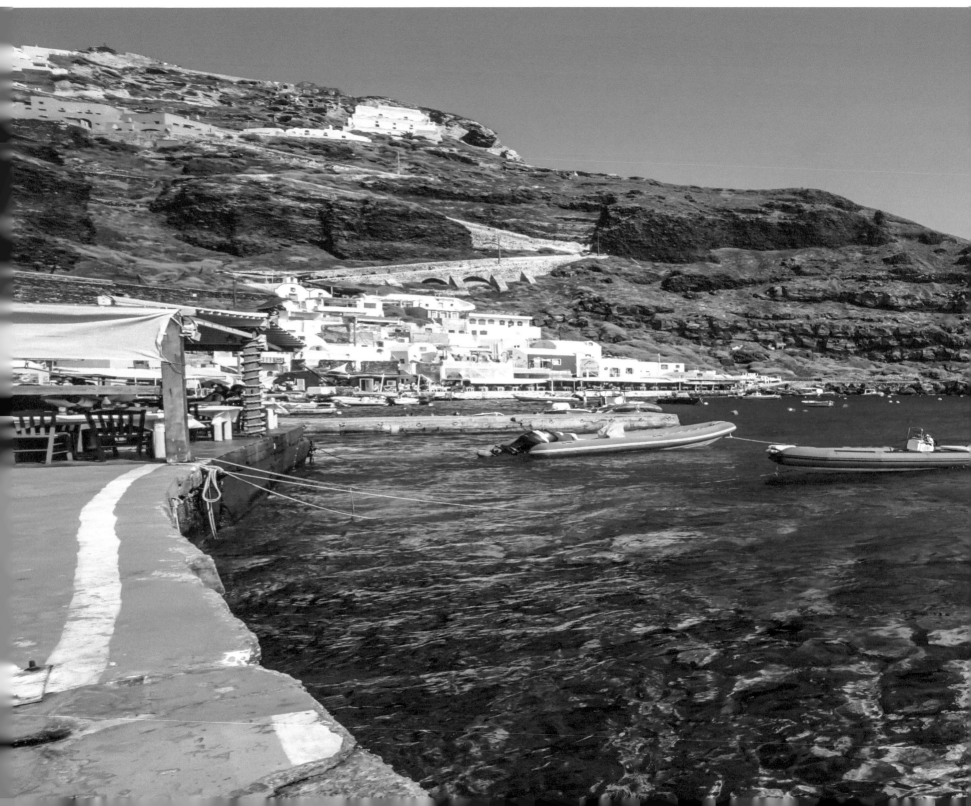

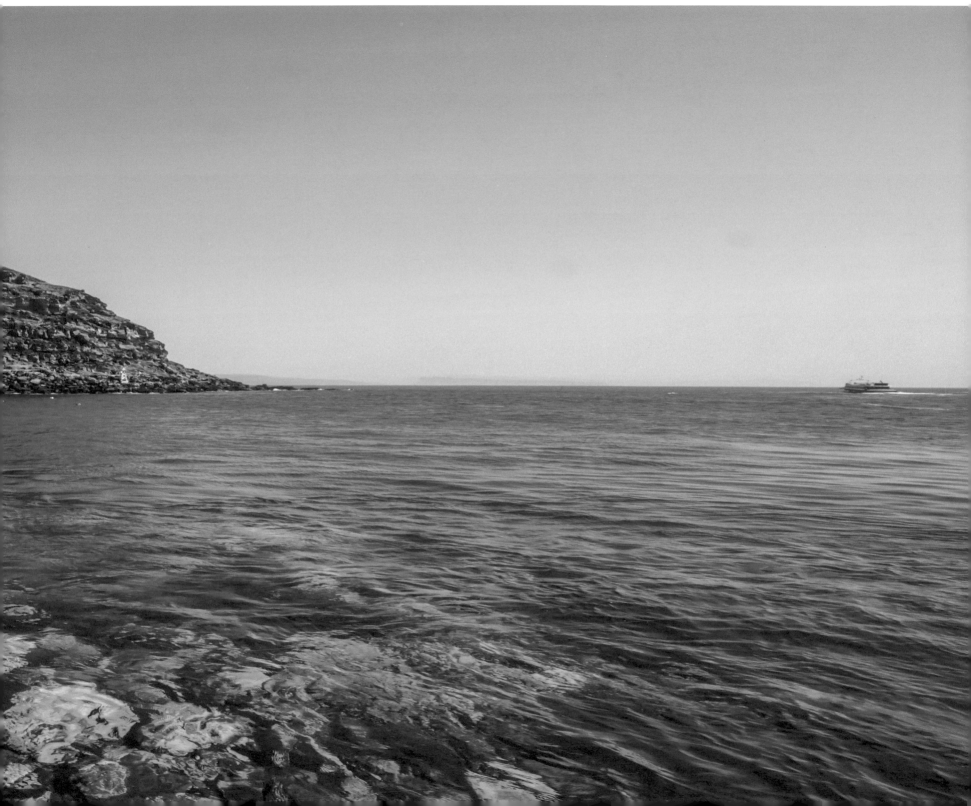

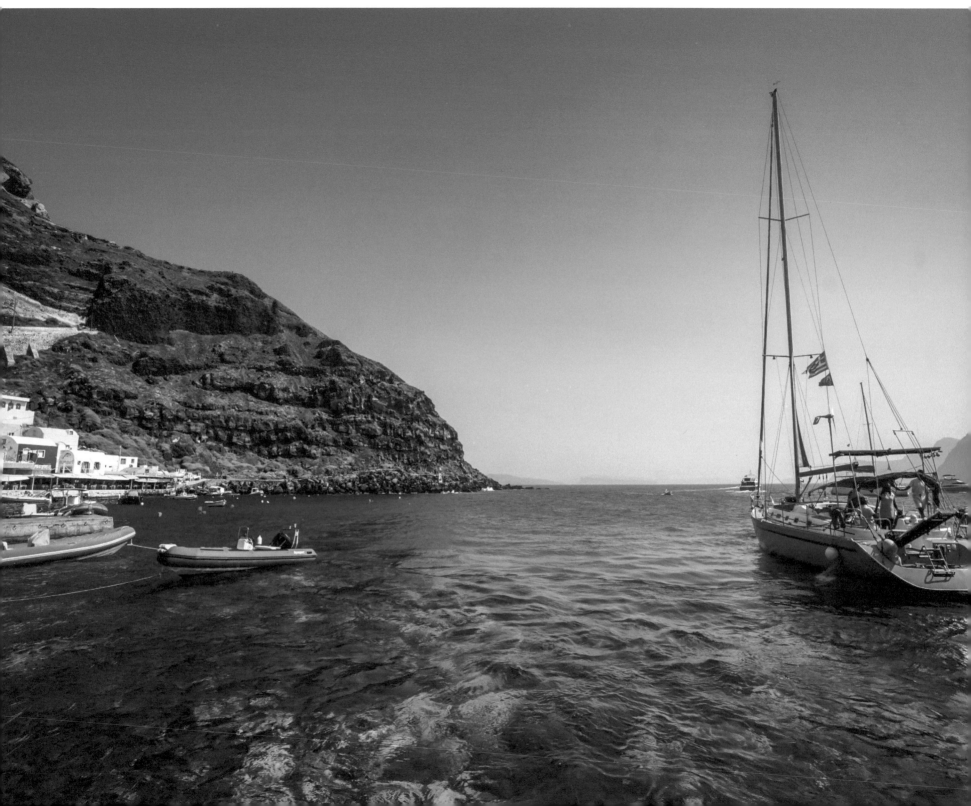

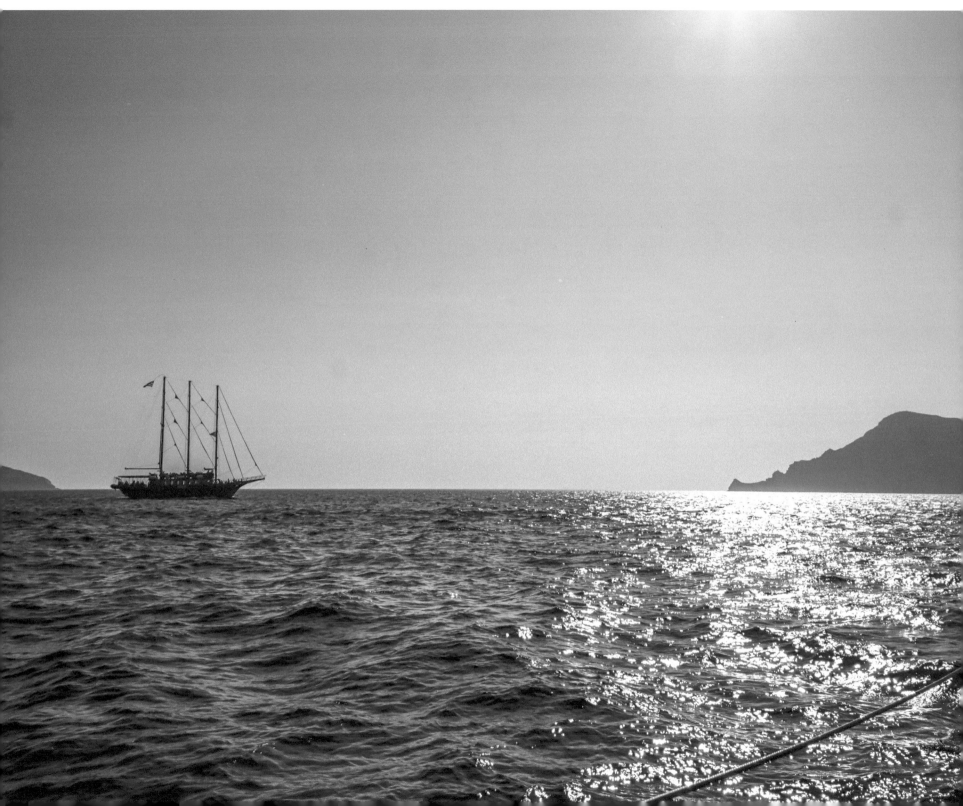

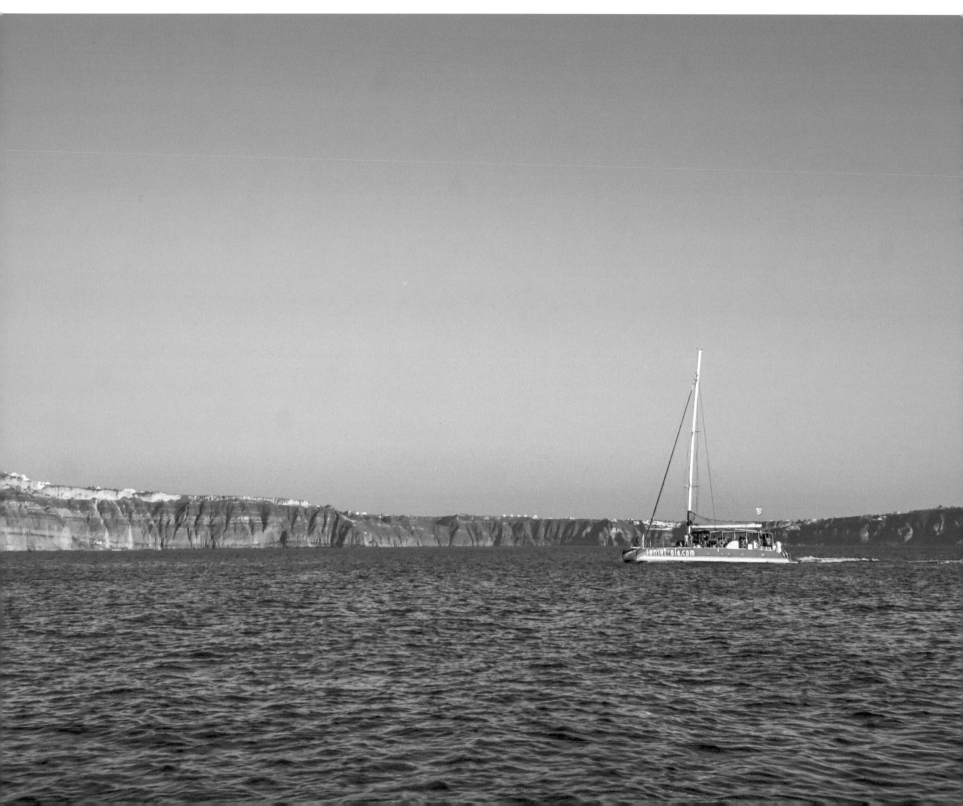

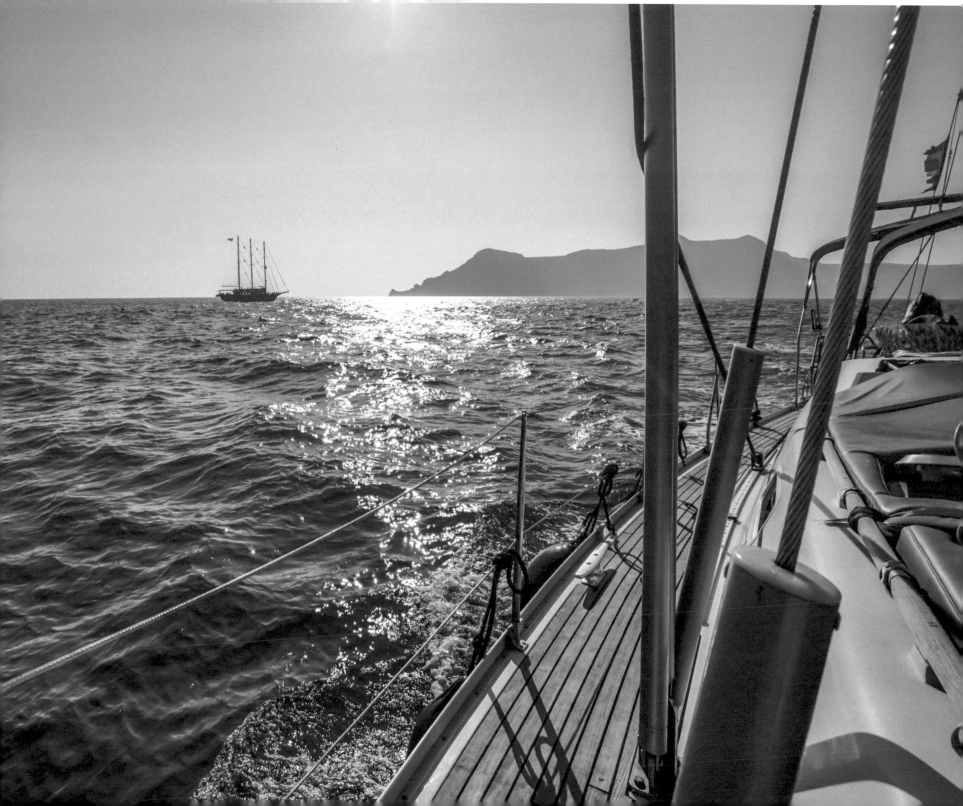

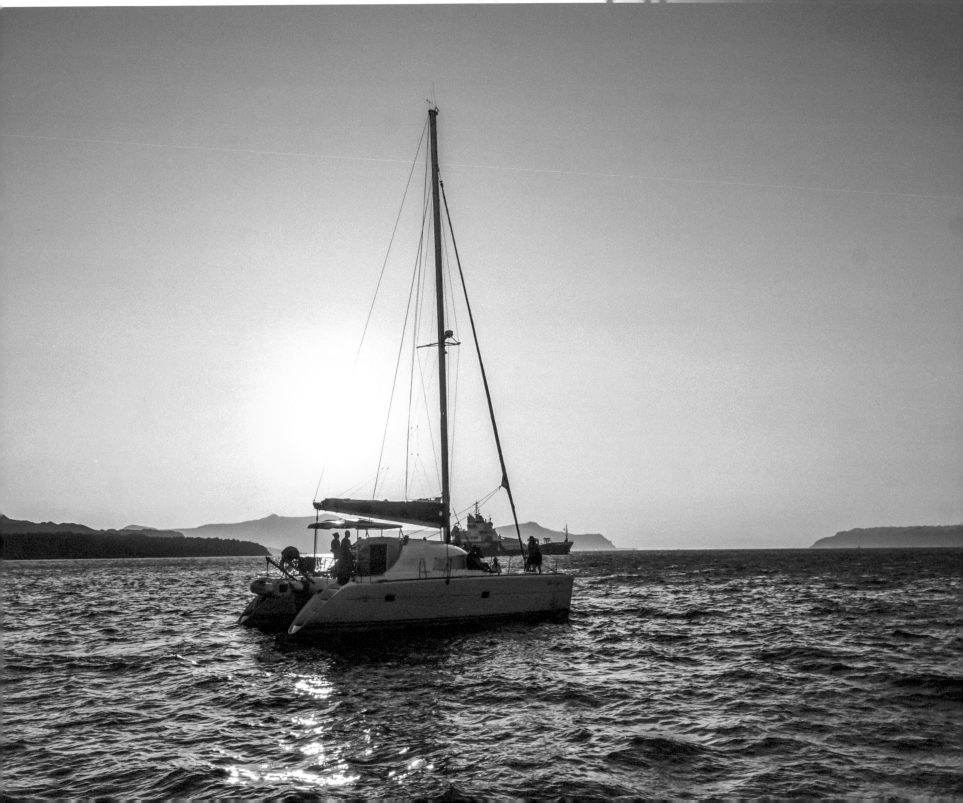

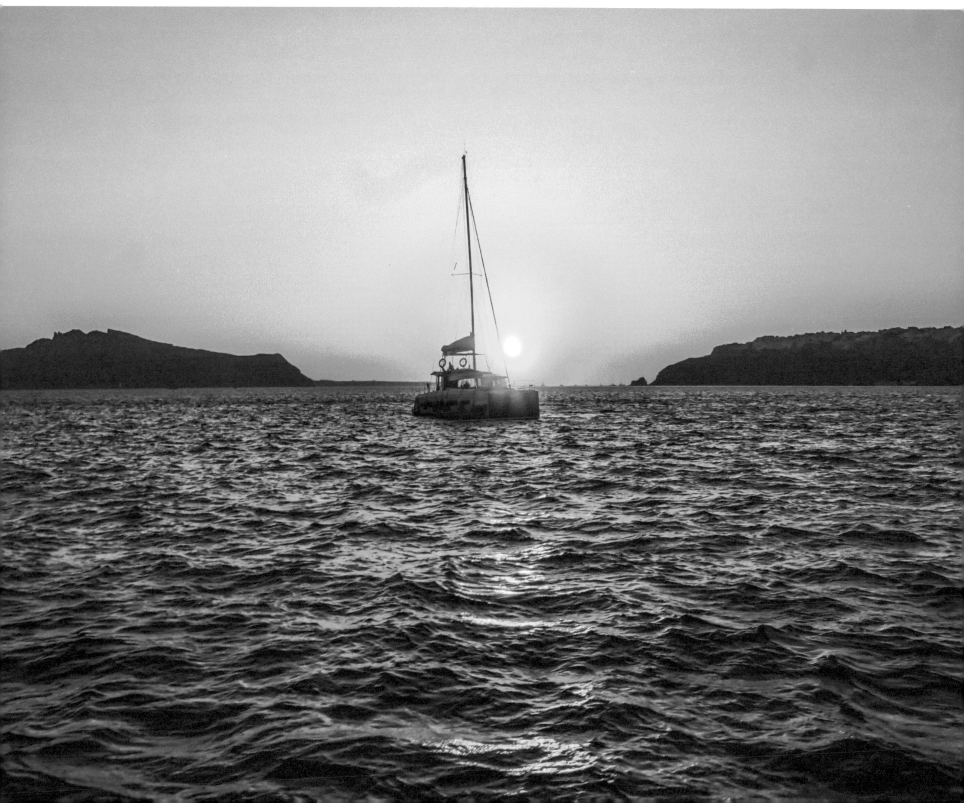

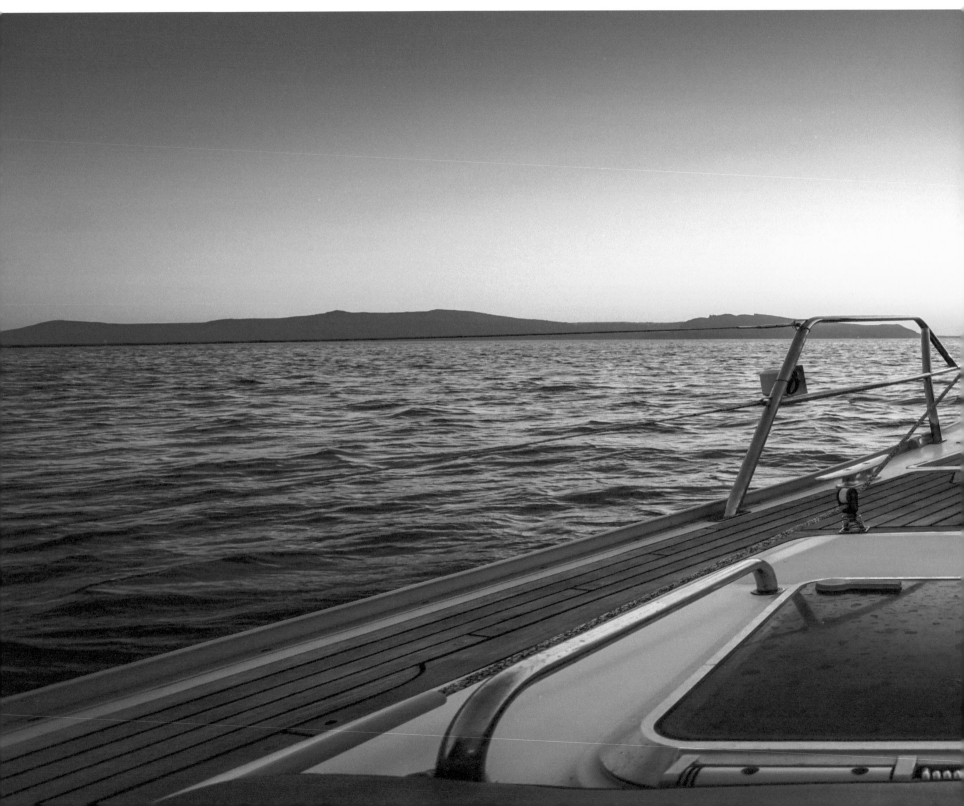

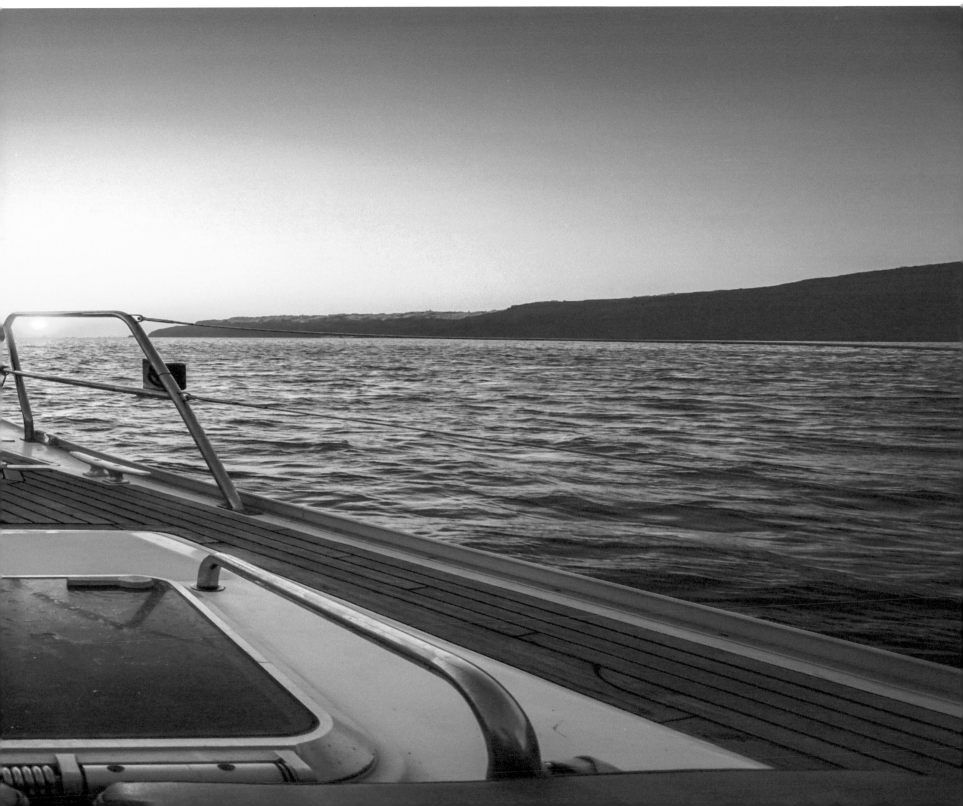

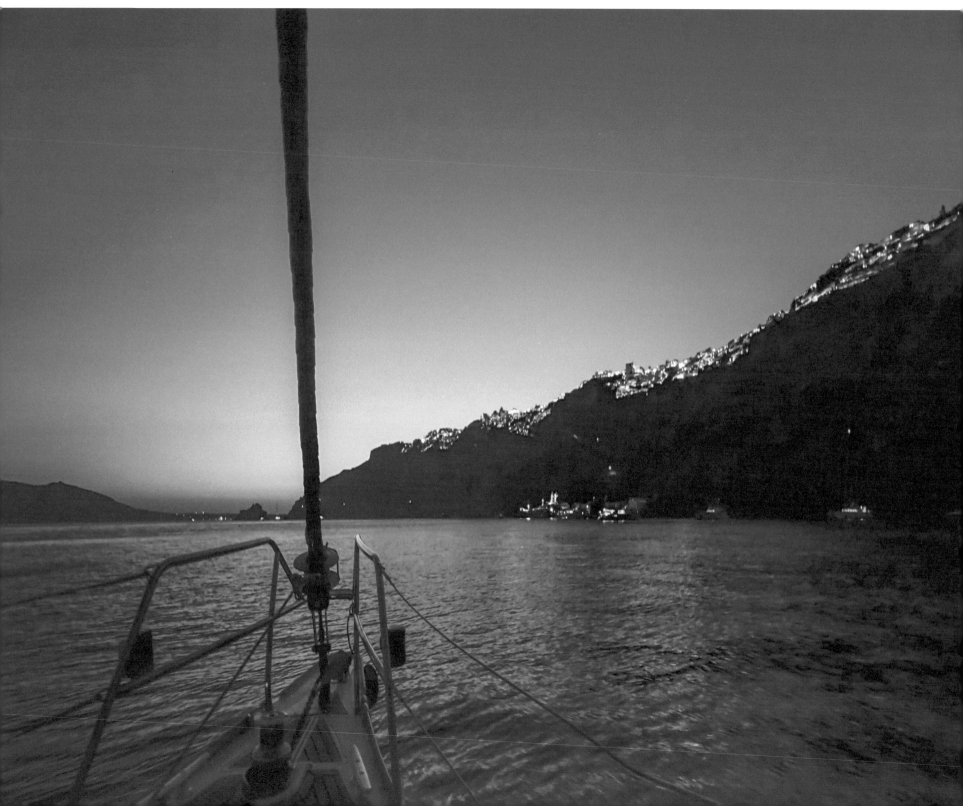

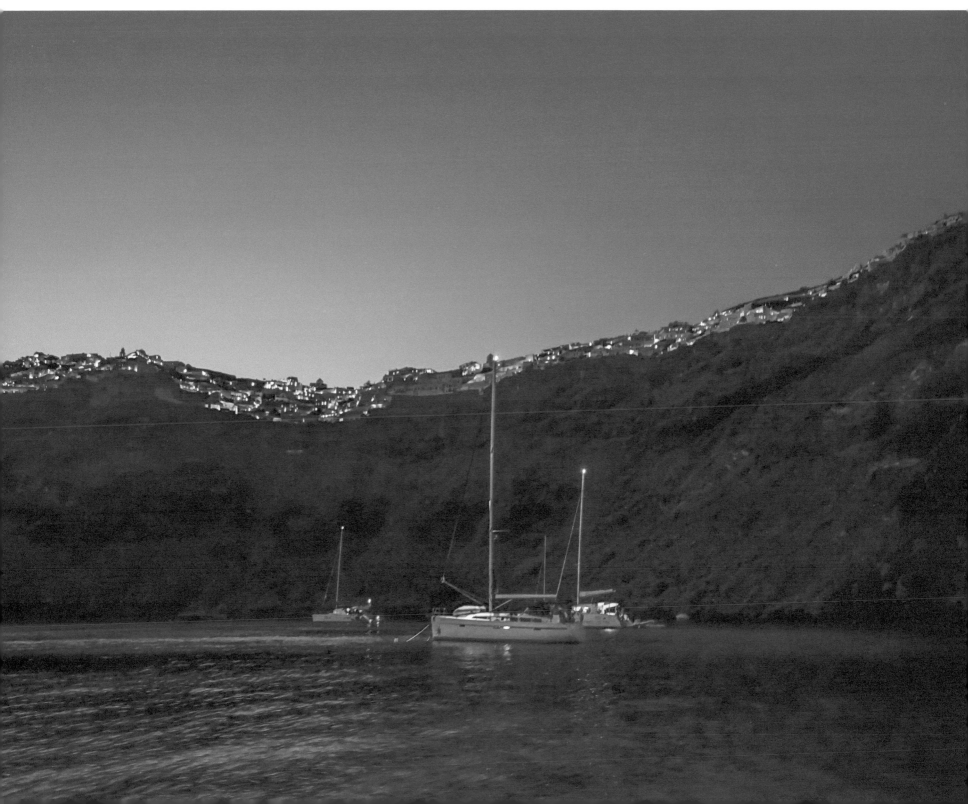

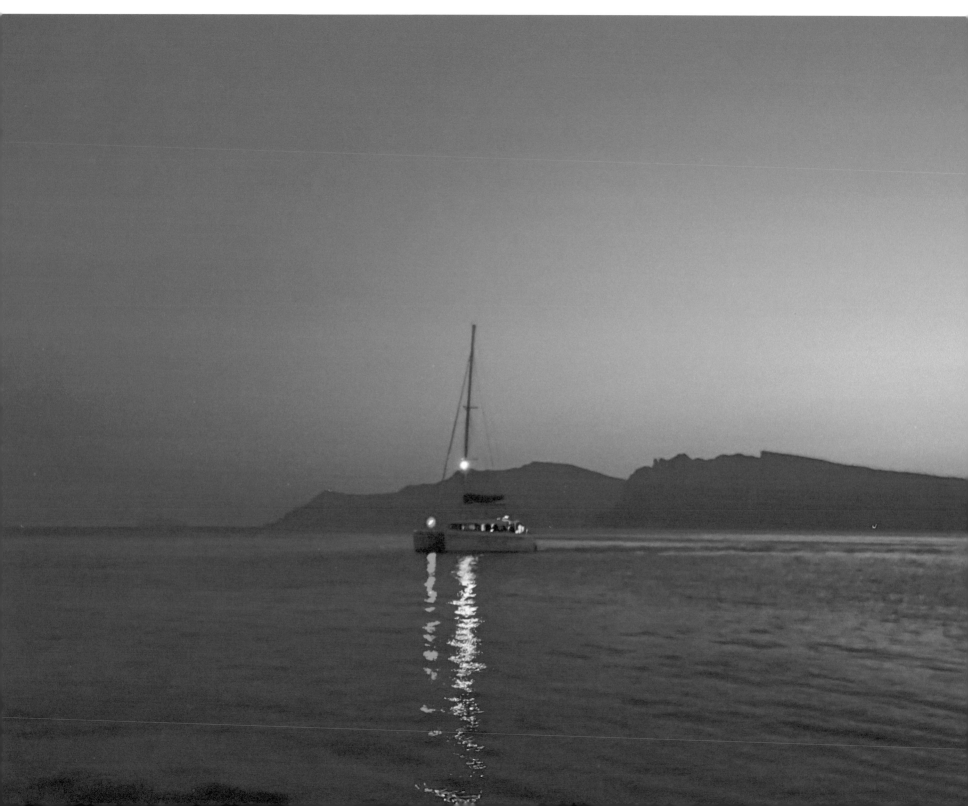